Paul James was born in Kingston-upon-Hull and joined
the Merchant Navy as a junior engineering officer.
During his 12 years' service he witnessed an enormous
change in both the vessels and the service conditions.
He obtained first-class steam and motor certification
before leaving the Merchant Navy for a career in ship
surveying. His first book, *A Ship So Far*, was published
by The Book Guild in 2000. Still 'sailoring on', the
author lives in Beverley, Yorkshire.

By the same author:

A Ship So Far, The Book Guild Ltd, 2000

A SEA SO DEEP

More Seaman's Tales

Paul James

The Book Guild Ltd
Sussex, England

First published in Great Britain in 2002 by
The Book Guild Ltd
25 High Street
Lewes, East Sussex
BN7 2LU

Typesetting in Times by
SetSystems Ltd, Saffron Walden, Essex

Printed in Great Britain by
Athenaeum Press Ltd, Gateshead

A catalogue record for this book is
available from the British Library

ISBN 1 85776 677 6

INTRODUCTION

A sea so deep,
A harbour that's near,
A good night's sleep, maybe . . .

Christmas 1963 should have been quite memorable for some really meaningful reasons. I was home with family and friends and not stuck on board a vessel berthed in some god-forsaken hot spot on the North African coast or, just as likely, freezing to death up the Bay of Fundy on the Canadian coast, pretending with those on board that life could be worse.

I recalled the previous Christmas in Sweden, not long after I had joined the *Lara* as Fourth Engineer. That had been something quite special and unique in my experience and probably wouldn't be repeated in a hurry.

I suppose if I was honest with myself, I was already missing my previous vessel and the shipboard contacts. The problem for me was that as most of my friends had entered the marriage stakes since I started my sea-going career, my local acquaintances were now a little thin on the ground. I missed the get-togethers and nights out but wasn't at all sure about striking up too close friendships, even with my new girlfriend in the south, until I knew what fate had in store for me in the immediate future. Most of the girls I had known previously weren't at all keen about one disappearing for months on end and then, on returning, expecting everything to be the same as before. I was definitely tempted to look up some former friends who I'd lost contact with but, in the end, I decided that discretion would be better than valour and accepted that at least for this Christmas duration, I would have to be content to eat well, drink in moderation and look forward to better things to come and returning south in the not too distant future.

After all, I decided, I had little to complain about. My sea-going career had taken me, so far, to North America, Pakistan, India, the central Mediterranean countries and finally Sweden, each proving to be vastly different in so many ways. The variety of ethnic cultures and religions, amongst many other things, made me ponder on how complex our human relationships are; little wonder that our attempts to understand each other's problems and difficulties are so often unsuccessful. At least with nature, it doesn't matter whether it's the Indian Ocean, Pacific Ocean, Western Ocean or the North Sea, the ocean's unpredictability is very much alike. A similar situation applies with the more fixed natural assets including the mountains, forests and plains, together with the fish, animals and birds that inhabit them, none of these being as individually identifiable by either their faults or failings as human beings are.

My thoughts frequently turned to some of the more eventful happenings of the previous few years of my career and, whilst I relished thoughts about the humorous occasions with both my ship-mates and the passengers, there were certain events which I certainly hoped wouldn't be repeated. After all, a collision at sea, in any circumstances, is not a happy or joyful occasion and tragic accidents with the loss of good friends are even more unpalatable.

Having said that, I still felt pretty certain that, based on my experiences to date, there were going to be a good few more surprises to come, with the probability of the odd disaster or two but hopefully of not too serious a nature.

Of one thing I was certain: I had no intention whatsoever of getting myself caught up in any more personal vendettas between the deck and engine room personnel, even if I incurred the wrath of those above me. By the same token, I was a great believer in mutual contact with the passengers if that was what they wanted, and sometimes they certainly did. After all, they had paid a not insignificant amount of money for the privilege of sharing our company as well as the vessel and, just occasionally, the attention they required didn't form part of the company's sales package.

Whether or not my next ship would take me to somewhere of incredible interest or banal boredom, only time would tell . . .

1

It soon became clear that there was no immediate requirement for me to join another vessel, so after the Christmas break I decided to try to get permission to return to college and continue my studies for the next part of my Certificate exams.

On many occasions it can be extremely difficult to obtain release from a vessel at the right time to start the course because, quite naturally, there are others with the same intentions and therefore it is quite possible that there is nobody available to relieve you. Having said that, it is important to start the course from the beginning and not try to catch up with those who attended from the start.

Fortunately, on this occasion, as I had been relieved from my vessel before Christmas, there was a clear route for me to follow to return to college. The only problem was that I had no transport to get me there.

After a bit of persuasion and until such time as I could take delivery of the car I had ordered before Christmas, my father agreed to my borrowing his car, provided I dropped him off at his city centre office each morning.

Each main port had its own faculty for teaching marine engineering, with a fair degree of competition to recruit students. I was lucky in one respect: my home was not too far distant from one of the best colleges whose recently retired head of the marine faculty had created a very sound academic base. They could also demonstrate a very successful pass rate amongst their students, which obviously generated a good turnover for them.

The thought of having one's feet on terra firma for a few months seemed an attractive prospect but other thoughts about the hard mental grind of intensive study followed by the turmoil in the exam room tended to put one right off the idea. It was always assumed by the college lecturers that you had already done a considerable amount of private study in advance of the course, so if, like me, you hadn't accomplished this, you were left with extremely intensive cramming sessions resulting in a mental daze.

Whilst at sea, there are occasions when you are called upon to perform beyond the normal call of duty and react in the most appropriate manner to suit the circumstances. In some instances, the action taken is to stabilise a dodgy situation, and this action has to be instantaneous and entirely predictable. Examiners are always looking to see if that type of situation is uppermost in your mind and that you are prepared to meet these sort of challenges, but actually performing in these situations as opposed to discussing them in an examination room is, of course, a vastly different scenario.

What really made life bearable was the spirit of bonhomie amongst those thrown into the boiling pot. Fortunately for us students, those that were doing the stirring really knew what they were doing. The chief stirrer for many of us was a genius whose speciality subject was engineering knowledge and whose artistic capability with a stick of chalk on the blackboard was almost legendary. His ability to create, on the blackboard, the innards of a fire tube boiler in almost the time it took to blow one's nose never failed to induce an almost trancelike state in the minds of the beholders.

His artistic genius was almost matched by his verbal dexterity as he explained the workings of his exquisitely reproduced mechanisms. I was frequently left feeling like a nodding toy strung in a car window, as I made great efforts to try to reproduce the same drawings in my notebooks at the same time as following his explanations whilst he pointed to the blackboard to illustrate the points he was making.

If artistic and verbal dexterity were the hallmarks of our EK lecturer, there was no way he could compete with our chemistry lecturer for sheer visual impact and explosive, ear-splitting dialogue. These were not particularly welcome attributes, as many had previously found to their cost. In fact, on entering the chemistry lecture room, there was always a mad dash to get a seat at the back if possible, if only to try and protect one's hearing and to avoid being splattered by liberal quantities of saliva from his flailing lips. There was always the possibility that one would emerge from the lecture room looking like the abominable snowman, covered in chalk dust spread in all directions by his more than liberal use of the blackboard duster or, even worse, accidentally clobbered by an uncontrolled swing of an arm being used to try and restore his balance after performing a passable imitation of a downhill skier.

But I suppose it was the practical experiments that he created for us that caused the most concern. What should have turned out to be as predictable as night following day was never quite like that as far as our dear Edwin's performances were concerned.

'If only ...' he would start to say. Then what would follow was nothing short of a diatribe about his poor assistant's lack of careful preparation or inaccurate measuring of the chemicals used, in fact just about everything that Edwin could summon up to explain the misfortune that surrounded his experiments. On occasions when he realised that something was going diabolically wrong, he would excuse himself from our presence, leaving us to wonder what our fate was going to be. He would then return just in time to wield whatever weapon was necessary to restore some semblance of normality to the scene and just once, the only effective weapon turned out to be a fire extinguisher. Even his simple experiment to show the effect of rusting of nails was doomed to failure. He explained that his assistant must have placed stainless steel nails inside the sealed jam jars instead of the usual variety.

Another of our lecturers, a serious young chap, took a

fair degree of pleasure in testing our knowledge and verbal responses to his deep and penetrating questions. I did my best to avoid his attention as some of his more demanding theory left me grasping at straws.

We were also being severely mentally challenged by the new developments in the latest technology. The idea was put forward that all these clever pieces of equipment were designed to make everyone's life a lot easier both on the bridge and in the engine room. Needless to say, there was a fair degree of scepticism about these claims but, in any event, we were expected to understand both the theory and the practice of these wonders of man.

Once again, my social life was taking a beating.

The intensity of the study increased as the days rolled on. There was never sufficient time to cover the full syllabus and, even living at home, it was a case of all work and no play. I often thought that a lot was expected from us in a relatively short period of time.

Then, out of the blue, I was contacted by a motoring organisation to see if I would be prepared to film their next event. The venue was only about 50 miles from home and I couldn't resist the temptation to repeat earlier such ventures.

I decided to take a day off from college to have a look at the circuit and work out the best camera locations. Although my cine camera had a three-lens turret providing telephoto, wide angle and normal shot lens, I did not have a zoom capability, therefore it was vital to make sure that the camera locations would yield plenty of local action. My decision to give the circuit a once-over proved extremely wise. As usual the race days proved hectic and demanding from a filming point of view, but exciting and enjoyable.

Once that brief interlude was over, it was back to business as usual.

My parents saw little of me as I kept my head down,

becoming a bookworm, and their conversation with me on some days amounted to,

'Your tea's ready, Paul, you'd better come right away otherwise it will be cold before you eat it.'

What sometimes drove my mother into a near frenzy and almost to breaking point were the telephone enquiries for me.

'It's for you again, dear. Sounds like a blonde bombshell to me,' she would say.

'Can't be, mum, I don't know any,' I would counter.

'For heavens sake, are you coming to the phone or not?' she pleaded.

'No, Mum, I'm not. If I don't get this work finished tonight, I'll be sunk. So, whoever it is who can't live without me, just tell her I'm not in.'

'Don't be so foolish, Paul, she knows you're in, she can hear your voice.'

'Hell, tell her I'm on the loo, suffering acute abdominal pains and sickness, not likely to survive – anything for God's sake.'

I don't think it took many more words from my mother for the poor lass to realise that she was wasting her time. Afterwards my mother would appear in my room.

'Look, Paul, how many more times do I have to tell you that I'm fed up of playing your fairy godmother. In future you will come to the phone and tell them why you're too rude to have a few words with them.'

'Mum,' I'd say, 'I'm terribly sorry, I don't mean to put you through all this hassle but I know that if I answer the phone, I'll end up going out and not doing any study, then I'll fail as sure as hell.'

'All right,' my mum would reply, 'just this time then. But can't you just simply tell them that you're not available at present? Quite honestly, though, it wouldn't do you any harm at all to have a few nights' break from all this study.'

As far as my father was concerned, provided he got his chauffered drive to work each day, I could stay at college until the cows came home and, if that meant a few exam failures helped by too much socialising along the way, then he'd fully agree with my mum that I did need to strike a balance.

'After all,' he would say, 'all work and no play makes for a very dull day.'

2

The examinations for the second part of the certificate I was sitting were intended to enable the successful candidate to sail as a second engineer on a steamship. However, at that time, if one could demonstrate sufficient knowledge of the particular vessel you were sailing on as a third engineer, and the owners could satisfy the Ministry of Transport that they had no certificated engineer available, then it was possible for a permit or dispensation to be conferred on the engineer applicant. Very stringent requirements were laid down with a view to preventing abuse of this relaxation of the certification regulations, and a dispensation usually only allowed a single voyage to be undertaken.

One of the ironies of the permit and dispensation schemes was the likelihood of the successful applicants being allowed to sail on the most popular voyages and the best vessels, simply because these voyages were of short duration. This often counted a great deal for the married officers, therefore the rewards for obtaining one's certificate by written examination as opposed to verbal assessment sometimes caused a fair degree of anguish, particularly if the newly certificated engineer was offered, as his reward, promotion on a vessel bound for the Indian Ocean with the likelihood of being away for many months.

The examinations I was involved with proved to be just as difficult as I had imagined they would be and, whilst I was extremely disappointed to find out that I had failed both sections I had sat, I wasn't too surprised at the result. Probably my dear mum was right, I was trying too hard and should have given myself more time off to relax and enjoy life once in a while.

It was suggested to me that I should re-sit the examinations again as soon as possible, otherwise all the efforts I had made and the study leave I had taken would be wasted. I suppose it was a case of good fortune favouring the brave because at my next attempt, whilst still going down on one section of mainly theoretical knowledge, I succeeded in passing the engineering knowledge section, which, naturally enough, pleased me enormously.

There was no doubt at all in my mind that I would really have to try to find more time to study at sea because the time allocated at college was just simply not enough to cover the massive syllabus laid down and the work required.

At least, having achieved some measure of further success, I didn't feel that it had all been a waste of time, although the company were not too enamoured with my efforts and rewarded me with marching orders to join the *Dorado* in London as Fourth Engineer. This vessel was one of several of a class that sailed to the Eastern Mediterranean and carried mainly cargoes of fruit and vegetables back to London. I hadn't previously come into contact with this class of vessel and I couldn't help but be conscious of the ancient mariner atmosphere that lingered about on board, an almost genteel air of bygone days, more reminiscent of sail. One particular feature of these vessels was the split accommodation area, with the deck officers' and passengers' cabins being located forward of the funnel, and the engineers' cabins located in a separate deck house aft of the funnel. Whilst these vessels were of the four cargo hold type, looking from the shore, they appeared to mainly consist of superstructure and accommodation with the crew's cabins being located in a further deck house and below deck at the aft end.

Whilst some of the officers were living in the south to be close to the UK arrival port, the Chief Engineer still maintained his home in the north but had a flat in London for convenience. He was not slow in reminding us all that if we couldn't enjoy ourselves ashore in London with all it had to offer then we had no hope elsewhere. London, at that time, was swinging in many different directions, the dockland areas were no exception. The Isle of Dogs was famous for, among other things, its pubs with entertainment on offer that even attracted hordes of folk from the West End.

Equally as famous as the pubs were the dockers whose speciality was the ability to stop work at the drop of a hat without warning or good reason. Their leader at that time was a gentleman called Jack Dash whose persistence and success in his chosen path of righteousness, captured the hearts and minds of dockers on a nationwide scale. There was simply no stopping him; he knew exactly what he was doing to restore the rights of the British dockers and ensure a prosperous future for them. Unfortunately, dear Jack could see no further than his nose end. When a national TV network took him on an expenses-paid trip to Antwerp to make a filmed record of what his Belgian counterparts were up to, he chose to ignore, or hadn't noticed, their highly efficient methods of operation or their diligence and dedication to sound working practices, which meant that ship-owners were choosing to discharge and load their vessels at this port rather than in the London dock system.

When he was asked to comment on this, Jack simply evaded the question and trotted out his stock phrases about the way British working men, and in particular dockers, were being treated. Of course, there was a good deal of truth in his claims about unfair treatment and poor financial reward, on occasions, for their efforts. Unfortunately, by using the protection afforded to them by the National Dock Labour Board Scheme, guaranteeing a docker a job for life regardless of his efforts, the country felt that blackmail was the order of the day. If the average docker had realised the sheer bedlam their actions as a whole were causing, and the damage they were doing to their own cause, then just maybe they would not have been led like lambs to slaughter.

9

The effect of the dockers' actions on ourselves was, at times, almost catastrophic. Sailing times were being continually changed, which wreaked havoc with our repair and maintenance schedules, often resulting in complete cancellation of necessary work as well as non-completion of other work started. Our leave and off-duty schedules were similarly affected and many of the crew were totally disillusioned by all the upheavals the dockers' actions were causing them. What really got out backs up was the fact that we were signed on ship's articles with stringent penalties for any of us who breached them, whereas the dockers could almost get away with murder without incurring any penalty whatsoever.

Talking of murders, there was one element of the population who made the dockers seem like angels in comparison. The hoodlums who, by day or night, were forever present in the dockland neighbourhood. Gang warfare prevailed on a scale reminiscent of Chicago in its heyday, but provided you recognised when your presence was no longer required in certain watering holes and you left when required, that was the closest encounter you or the average person in the street would have with the hoodlums and their minders.

Just down the road from the Isle of Dogs was Chinatown, with eating establishments providing food of quality and abundance which could surely only be matched in its country of origin. Evidence of their success could be simply seen by the sheer number of patrons present in the numerous venues. My first visit to one, chosen by our Chief Engineer and a couple of the other officers from our vessel, proved to be not only a mouth-watering event but very much an eye-watering spectacle, certainly as far as I was concerned. My knowledge of Chinese food was virtually nil and the Chief suggested I try one of the curry specials as a starter. After only one mouthful, I just managed to exclaim, 'What the hell ...' before my throat was consumed by a ball of fire which I could only extinguish with a couple of glasses of water fortunately strategically at hand. Since that time, despite not having problems with any other items on a Chinese menu, I'm still as wary as ever when it comes to eating curries of any origin.

3

Just when I thought I was going to be able to take a train from London to Kent to visit my relations and girlfriend during the last weekend before we were due to sail, right out of the blue I was ordered to return north. I was being replaced by another engineer but there was no explanation immediately forthcoming for this sudden change of events. Apart from the obvious disappointment of not being able to do what I'd hoped to, I was more than a little concerned about the reasons for these orders.

After returning north and reporting to the company's offices, I discovered to my amazement that I had been incorrectly assigned to the *Dorado* and that instead I was being promoted to Third Engineer on the *Leo*, which also sailed out of London. Quite naturally I was not only relieved to find out that I'd not blotted my copy book but was actually looking forward to rejoining a vessel I'd sailed on before and knew well.

What I also hoped to find was the same atmosphere on board as I had experienced previously, but on joining the vessel a week later, I was soon to discover that our Chief Engineer had significant drink-related problems and the Second Engineer had given up on the opposite sex after several unhappy experiences. The Fourth Engineer was a Yorkshireman from the West Riding; despite being recently divorced, he was far from giving up on various ladies in his life who appeared to have played a significant part in his divorce. The deck officers, by comparison, were relatively sane and normal, with the Second Mate having a great sense of humour, if somewhat misguided at times.

On the night before we sailed and at his suggestion, we both ventured ashore and made our way to a local pub on the Mile End Road near the Blackwall Tunnel, where, he had been told a group with a difference appeared. As we entered the establishment, the refrains of Nancy Sinatra's 'These Boots are Made for Walking', together with powerful guitar rhythm and percussion accompaniment, reverbrated in our ears. The melody was being sung by a female but on entering the entertainment lounge, we could scarcely believe our eyes. The entire group was female and they were not only performing in a brilliant manner but were scarcely wearing any garments, at least below their navels. The place was packed out with the males transfixed by the most resplendent display of exquisitively shaped females thighs that one could imagine. The boots they were wearing were hardly noticed.

The Second Mate belatedly discovered his voice. 'For heaven's sake, Paul, I've got bigger trouser belts than the skirts these lasses are wearing.'

'They certainly give good value for money in every sense. It's the first time I've come across an all-female group but I'll be back for more next time we're back in London,' I replied.

'Me too, Paul, but as I've an early turn to in the morning, I fancy heading back to the ship. We could drop in to the Bricklayers Arms for a final pint, if you like,' he suggested.

This pub was only a short walk to the dock, and during the day it was used by all and sundry. But on a night time a visit might result in unpredictable situations, depending on the clientile inside or arriving after you. What none of us realised at that time was the unscrupulous nature of some of the individuals who frequented the East End hostelries. The Kray brothers' presence was certainly being felt by many, but neither of us dreamt that we would very shortly be personally confronted with their acquaintances, and that was entirely my fault.

'Yes, OK, Dave, let's do just that. After all, we're quite likely going to have to put up with warm beer once at sea.'

There was not the slightest hint of anything untoward as we entered the lounge, with the juke box belting out the latest pop hit. After being served, we just sat and stared into space as discussion was impossible.

The music stopped and a young man moved over to the juke box to choose another selection, but he'd not even reached it when a raucous voice called out, 'No more, young man, tonight.'

The voice didn't belong to the landlord, whose face was clouded with anxiety.

As the young man didn't respond as invited to, he was grabbed by a couple of minders and thrown out of the pub.

'For your information, you lot, we're having an important meeting in the next room, so don't switch that bloody machine on again, OK?'. The speaker was extremely well dressed, more like a businessman, but the malevolance in his voice was unmistakable.

When the speaker had disappeared into the next room, the landlord made his way over to us.

'Our guests next door are not good news, I'm afraid. If I was you, I'd drink up and be on my way.'

'But who the hell do they think they are, coming in here and telling your customers what they can and can't do,' asked the Second Mate.

'Let's just say we're entertaining the twins tonight, gentlemen, and leave it at that, if you don't mind.' The anxiety had once again returned to his face and immediately I suggested to Dave that we beat a hasty retreat while the going was good.

Little were we aware of the havoc that these two brothers were creating, particularly amongst the criminal fraternity. Their protectionist rackets extended far and wide into the underworld, and many wished they'd never crossed swords with the infamous twins.

On returning to the vessel and after bidding goodnight to the Second Mate, I was greeted by the Second Engineer with the news that there had been a major boiler failure whilst I'd been ashore. Apparently it was caused by lack of care and attention by one of the shore staff who were employed in port to look after the engine room services for the vessel. It looked as if our departure would be delayed several days to enable repairs to be carried out, and this, in fact, turned out to be the case.

Eventually, after considerable efforts had been expended by all of the engine room staff, we were on our way. However, during the course of the Second Engineer's watch and whilst we were proceeding off the Goodwin Sands in the English Channel, problems once again developed, this time with the main engines. We had to stop the vessel to rectify faults which had come about as a result of some unsatisfactory repairs carried out in London. The Chief was cursing his luck, and the Captain was extremely concerned about our lack of propulsion power in such a dangerous location. Fortunately, we were able to carry out sufficient adjustments to the valve gear to enable us to resume the voyage. More repairs could be made at the next port of call.

I was still trying to adjust to the watchkeeping hours which I'd previously experienced as a junior engineer, but the thought of being awake from midnight until four in the morning day after day, was not an inviting prospect. At least the weather was very much in our favour, and as we headed south from the Bay of Biscay, the clear blue skies and brilliant sunshine restored my morale. I was hoping and praying that the main engines would not play up again before we reached Benghazi, as trying to carry out suitable repairs in open sea conditions was extremely difficult and somewhat hazardous with a vessel pitching and rolling.

Good fortune favoured us and, on arriving at Benghazi, our agent informed us that we would have four days to play about with our engines before the vessel was due to depart for Piraeus. As far as I was concerned, the agent couldn't have given us much better news because I would be providing much of the effort required to carry out our main engine repairs.

We were able to replace the defective parts with new spares and, despite the heat and humidity in the engine room, a satisfactory result ensued, much to the relief of the Chief Engineer. At least I felt that I'd justified my promotion in the most practical of ways but was acutely aware that it might not happen again when I was next called upon to try and remedy a problem of that proportion.

Our subsequent voyage to Piraeus proved to be entirely uneventful except that the Chief decided his liquid intake required to be stepped up because of the extreme heat. Most of the increased amount came from the bonded locker, which increased the Chief Steward's sales figures no end. Fortunately we had no passengers on this voyage, therefore his indiscretions passed without too much comment, and by the time we arrived at Piraeus the Chief had sobered up and was ready to meet the usual motley mixture of shore representatives who managed to find someone or something to represent.

4

As some form of reward for my sterling efforts at Benghazi, the Second Engineer proposed that he and I should take a trip up to Athens and take a look around the ancient monuments and the Acropolis. Although I wasn't too enthusiastic to share his company ashore as well as on board, I felt it would be more than churlish to turn down his proposal.

We departed by train for the relatively short journey into the city on the morning of our arrival, leaving the Fourth Engineer to pander to the needs of the Chief. Neither of us was at all sure where we should get off the train but on seeing a station marked Olympiad on the train map, we unaminously agreed it was well worth a try.

Our stunning intuition was amply rewarded, and as we headed out of the station, we were in no doubt whatsoever that we had certainly arrived at our chosen destination with a vista so awe-aspiring, words could hardly describe it.

It was made abundantly clear in the tourist brochures that this amazing city had survived more ordeals throughout its history than any other comparable city, with Greece itself no stranger to trouble and strife on a grand scale. Somehow or other, though, Athens and the nation as a whole seem to rise above the disasters, shrugging off the despair and destruction that has been the downfall of other civilisations caught up in similar events.

Probably the power above all others that has sustained and protected the Greek nation emanates from the immortal works of the writers and artists of ancient Greece. Yet before our very eyes was the real actual evidence of survival through the undoubted dramas of Greek history. The amazing Acropolis, towering in magnificent splendour on a rocky ridge on the south-west of the city, with the Parthenon summounting this Upper City, truly an epic survivor. In such surroundings, one is almost overwhelmed by the grandeur of the architecture and the length of time it has existed in relation to one's own existence on the face of the earth. The dazzling whiteness of the 46 Doric columns, whilst adding to the spectacle, reflected the sun's midday rays, and it was with some considerable relief that we entered the Acropolis Museum, the relative coolness within providing a welcome escape.

The museum houses ancient relics discovered in the various excavations carried out on the Acropolis over many years, together with statues and plaster casts and, quite incredibily, fragments from the original Parthenon frieze created by Phidias and his pupils.

On the southern slope of the Acropolis, we found the Odeon of Herodes Atticus, a music ampitheatre built in the style of a Roman theatre with seating originally for 5,000 patrons. It was now used, so we were told, for performances of ancient drama by the Greek National Theatre and concerts by the Athens State Orchestra. In addition, the Athens Festival was held there, with both Greek and foreign artists and orchestras performing.

Although the whole scene that lay before us was truly impressive, neither of us could claim to be little more than interested bystanders, and after a short while we escaped to the lower slopes. But we could not leave without seeing the Stadium Olympieum, originally built in 330 BC then faced in white marble by Herodes Atticus in the 2nd century AD, with seating for about 50,000 spectators. The length of this stadium was about 770 feet and the actual course 600 Greek feet and marked by four Hermes statues. The modern stadium, inaugurated in 1896 with the first modern Olympic Games, was built as closely as possible to the original design, which was found in the excavations together with two of the Hermes statues, and these were used, once more, to mark the modern course.

We made our way to the foot of the Acropolis hill and into the district known as The Plaka. Its narrow streets, old mansions and houses, its picturesque taverns and jasmin bushes and basil pots in the courtyards, together with the flower pots on the window sills, make The Plaka one of the most idyllic and captivating quarters of Athens. It is claimed that when the old cantatas (songs of old Athens) are heard escaping the tavern walls, it is as though the Athens of the centuries gone by was still alive in the narrow twisting streets. None of the performers were present during our visit but the relief for our aching tired limbs was most welcome as we partook of cool liquid refreshment in our chosen tavern.

It was only after we had returned to the vessel and I was reflecting on what we had seen that the enormity and scale of the everlasting architecture truly sank in. Probably no other country could proudly display its history in such a tangible form, apart from Egypt.

I didn't have too long to reflect on such thoughts because of more pressing matters needing attention in the engine room once more. I couldn't help but think that a lot of routine maintenance had not been carried out for some time and this neglect was more than likely the reason for the repetitive problems that were occurring. There didn't seem to be an overabundance of enthusiasm amongst those on board to attempt to improve the situation to any significant extent, although the Fourth Engineer shared my own concern about these problems and we tried to work out a limited schedule between ourselves to tackle the more pressing ones.

We did manage to depart from Piraeus on schedule, bound for Messina for bunkers, and it seemed like sheer heaven to be able to leave the bunkering in the Fourth Engineer's hands and retire gracefully from the scene.

The Second Mate had suggested a walk ashore into the city after our arrival as there was no cargo working. Like me, he couldn't wait to exercise his legs and put a bit of distance between himself and the vessel.

'You know Paul, it's a hell of a time since I've sailed with such a miserable crowd. The Old Man's a perfect pain in the backside. He's only here for three trips so I don't know what he's moaning about. The Mate is continually complaining about being overlooked for promotion because he's never in the right place at the right time, which is probably true. As for the Third Mate, he's just come off the Scandinavian service and is very much missing the home comforts, so to speak.'

'Well, I can sympathise with the Third Mate. I also sailed not so long ago on the Scandinavian service and the difference in the vessels and the conditions has to be experienced to be believed. As you know, the Chief's fine when he's sober, the Second's got one hell of a chip on his shoulder with regard to his past amorous adventures which seems to keep him permanently depressed and there's only the Fourth who's ready for action, although I get the feeling he'd rather have his action ashore and preferably in the bed of some damsel in distress.'

We'd entered a local tavern about midway between the harbour and the city centre and ordered the usual drinks, local brew of choice quality.

'Dave, I don't know about you but I have a feeling of déja-vu. Just like when we were sitting in the Bricklayers Arms in London before we sailed.'

'You mean those agitated-looking so-and-sos sitting at the bar who seem unduly interested in us two.'

'Yes. Also the barman, who looks as if he's just messed himself. Come on, for heaven's sake, let's drink up and be on our way before we get involved in their no doubt bloody affairs.'

It was only a short while later when glancing at a newspaper in the post office that we discovered that there was a war being fought out in the back streets of the city between the local Mafia gangs, and we had obviously not timed our visit to the tavern all that well. If we had appreciated at that time the ferocity and anger of the warring parties, I don't think we'd even have stepped ashore. The ruthless nature of the vendettas meant innocent bystanders could easily be caught in the crossfire of the gangsters.

The homeward voyage proved to be relatively uneventful and there was no regret when we eventually berthed in the London docks, with reliefs awaiting our arrival.

I had intended to take a few days' break in Kent and renew my aquaintance with my girlfriend but I received news that my new car was awaiting collection, therefore I had to return north to take delivery.

5

I could barely wait to get home and appear at the Rootes Group main dealer showrooms. Although the new model I was acquiring was the same model as the one I'd previously disposed of, there were some fundamental design changes, particularly concerning the rear end, which some people thought would result in the model losing its distinctive appearance. The new model had a larger and more powerful engine although the overdrive arrangements had been dispensed with. As soon as I saw the car, I was certain the designer had made the right decision but the proof would only be demonstrated if a balanced on-road performance was forthcoming.

After the usual exchange of paperwork and confirming with the salesman that the car was exactly as ordered, I finally departed, feeling, like the driver of any brand new vehicle, apprehensive but exceedingly excited. Testing the performance would have to wait until the engine and transmission were run in but the positive feel and handling, particularly on roundabouts and winding roads close to home, left me in no doubt whatsoever that my new Sunbeam Alpine was going to provide me with many hours of on-road pleasure.

On arriving home, I was surprised to see my father's car parked on the road and the garage doors open. He had anticipated that I would want to place my new car under cover, but whilst that would have been my preferred option, the continual changing round of both cars was not at all practical, so it was agreed that whilst I was at home, my car would remain outside.

My mother was, as usual, not slow to see the significant advantage for my social position.

'Paul, while you were away last time, I had the usual calls from your female admirers enquiring about your whereabouts. I remember one in particular, a girl called Diane. She seemed very anxious to speak to you. I remember her mentioning something new happening in her life. You never know, your new car might just prove to be another new happening for her.'

Once again, my dear mum's logic left me wondering what the hell she was trying to get at.

'OK Mum, just to satisfy your curiosity, I will try to contact Diane, but she might not even be living at her address.'

I had to admit, I was more than a little curious as to why she'd suddenly sprung out of the woodwork, so to speak, as it was quite some time since our paths had last crossed.

Diane actually was quite some girl. I'd met her out of the blue at a local dance held in a city centre ballroom and first noticed her when I was sitting at a nearby table.

I glanced up to notice an attractive brunette apparently being pestered by an extremely inebriated old fool making his presence more than uncomfortably obvious to one and all. He didn't appear to want to take no for an answer and, as the dance was a general excuse-me waltz, I took off on a mission impossible and whisked her onto the dance floor under his very nose, just hoping his reaction would prove to be less than hostile.

'Thanks, really truly thanks. I was imagining myself trying to cope with him on the dance floor in his present condition.' She then smiled. 'I'm Diane and you're . . .?'

'Paul,' I answered. 'Oh, it was nothing. Are you with anyone, if you don't mind me asking?'

'No,' she replied. 'I'm not local, well not any more. I live and work in London as a secretary but just pop home, once in a while, to see my folks. How about you?'

23

I told her about my seagoing career and that I was visiting the dance hall for the first time, since it had opened fairly recently. We agreed the place was quite impressive but weren't quite so sure about the clientele, certainly on that evening. We chatted on, had a few drinks and near the end I offered her a lift home, which she accepted.

'I don't have to be home by one a.m., you know, Paul. How about a little drive down to the foreshore. I think I can trust you.'

'That's fine by me,' I responded, and switched on the radio. Despite it being the end of July, it was far from being a perfect summer's evening. Nevertheless, I felt the warmth from the relative closeness of her presence and I continued telling her of my seafaring experiences.

'A girl in every port, I bet, Paul,' she murmured.

'Not quite,' I replied. 'In fact, to be honest, one spends almost as much time trying to escape the clutches of some of these frantic females as enjoying the company of their saner and safer compatriots.'

She told me about her family; her father was a business-man in the pickle line who supplied many of the city retail outlets and, by all accounts, wasn't short of a bob or two. We moved on to music, her top of the pops ... All this talking and listening was making me decidedly sleepy.

'I think it's time I got home now,' she said, apparently noticing my occasional failure to respond.

'Yes, sure thing, you point us in the right direction,' I suggested.

The directions she gave me were vaguely familiar but not quite leading to the select area I imagined would have been commensurate with a father of good fortune. Instead of heading out to the leafy select suburbs then into the nearby hilly surrounds where there was a plethora of magnificent mansions, we were going back towards the central area of the city.

'Next street on the left, Paul, then about halfway down.'

She directed me to stop outside a mid-Victorian terraced house in a somewhat dilapidated and run-down street only a stone's throw from the bright lights, hustle and bustle, yet here time could have stood still for half a century or more. Even the gas lights hadn't been altered and the broken bottles and litter strewn about did nothing to brighten up the scene.

'Come in for a coffee, if you like. There's only my father and sister at home. Mum's away on holiday with the rest of the family.'

'I really think I ought to be on my way, Diane . . .'

'Paul, you're not a kiddie wink. Your mum and dad aren't likely to spank your bottom if you're late, now are they?'

'No, that's very true. OK then. Just for a short while,' I added.

Her father was enormous, very hale and hearty and greeted me with 'Don't mind the pickle jars, lad, we're a bit short of space both here and in the factory.'

I struggled to get down the hallway, over the top of cases apparently full of brand new empty jars, and eventually reached his huge outspread waiting hand.

'Nice to meet you, son. Come on in. What's your poison?'

'Well, I don't mind, tea, coffee, whatever you have ready . . .'

'Nay, nay, son, I mean Scotch, gin, beer . . . you know.'

'Oh, right. A Scotch and ginger ale would be great.' I added, trying to adjust to his unexpected friendliness.

'Not a bad business mine, you know. I'm the top pickle man in this neck of the woods. Big turnover, a bit seasonal . . . too bloody competitive by far at the present time . . .'

He rambled on. Diane had disappeared. I was getting more than a trifle concerned that each time I reassured him that it was only his pickles I ate, he truly rewarded my allegiance by topping up my glass with ever diminishing quantities of ginger ale and increasing amounts of Scotch. I was fast reaching the point where driving my car was going to be impossible. It was no good, I simply had to excuse myself but I hadn't a clue how to. I felt trapped in more ways than one. His voice focused my dilemma once again.

'Well, my son, Diane's abandoned us. I'm ready for my

25

pit, got to be up at five a.m. so I'll bid you goodnight. You let yourself out when you've finished your drink, eh! Probably see you again.'

'Thanks, I've enjoyed myself very much. Yes, we'll no doubt meet again, goodnight.'

'Knowing my Diane,' he laughed, 'that'll be a sure fire certainty.'

He disappeared, leaving me wondering about this somewhat unusual family: a daughter who had escaped the overpowering onion environment, a mother who obviously did likewise when the need required, a father who thrived on pickled onions and precious little else, unseen motley brothers and sisters and a house and street that had seen many a better day.

My thoughts wandered momentarily to places abroad not all that much different from the place I was just about to leave.

6

'Paul, are you coming to the phone or not?' My mum once again, was on the receiving end of one of my calls. She thought it was the girl who had called while I was away.

'Yes, tell her I won't be a moment, please.' I struggled to leave the bathroom in some order of decency.'

'Diane, sorry about that. I was in the bathroom when you rang. Anyway, how are you? Long time, no see, I'm afraid. This wayward life of mine, you know,' I pleaded.

'All right, I suppose,' she answered. 'I thought you would have rung at least, to see if I was still alive.'

'Well, I presumed you'd returned to London. I don't have your telephone number or address in the south, you know,' I replied.

'Paul, straight out, do you like me or not?'

'Yes, of course I do, but just at the present time I seem to have more on my plate than I can cope with. As soon as I've got myself sorted out, I'd love to ask you out again.' That was partly true but I certainly wasn't going to say that I also found her family circumstances just a little bizarre and strange.

'If you really liked me, you wouldn't come up with that sort of excuse . . .' Then there was a click.

'Diane, Diane . . .' But she had rung off.

'Well,' said mum, 'what did you have to say to her?'

'Look, Mum, she's a very nice lass but her family seem a rum lot, although I could be wrong. Anyway, I'm not rushing into any more close entanglements for the time being. This vocation of mine wreaks havoc with personal relationships, and I've still got a lot of studying and college attendance to cope with for the time being, you know.'

'I bet you didn't try and explain things to her, now did you?'

'No, to be perfectly honest, I didn't, but we'll see,' I replied.

There were no more calls from her and before I knew it, it was time to return to London and rejoin my vessel.

Probably the best news that we could hear was that passengers would be boarding for the forthcoming voyage, this meant that the food would not only be edible, but of a varied nature. In other words, not pork served in every conceivable form but a choice of dishes as good as anything on offer in a pricey restaurant.

For once, our departure was not delayed by unforeseen circumstances, the weather was favourable and we headed off down the English Channel on our usual course, bound for the even warmer climes of the Mediterranean.

Our first port of call was Benghazi and instead of pursuing a lost cause in the gaming room of the Hotel Berenice along with their rich clientele, we accepted an invitation from the NAAFI to join their ranks for a party. This, of course, wasn't our first visit to the NAAFI. They seemed to welcome a change of face and that was a feeling mutually shared.

Our Second Engineer, being a former Naval serviceman, felt more than at home in obviously familiar surroundings and, for once, actually came to life in a social way and even allowed the chip to slip off his shoulder for an hour or two. It was hard to believe, sitting in the cool comfort of the NAAFI, enjoying very friendly hospitality, good food and as many drinks as one could accommodate, that out there, only just down the track beyond the tarmacadam roads, was an environment as hostile as any on the face of this earth of ours. An environment that needed a cool calm nerve to exist in, especially if things went wrong, and sheer guts and determination to survive, no matter what happened. Our service friends recalled incidents that had happened to them despite their usual careful planning and I, for one, preferred the vagaries of the sea conditions to the thought of frying in the heat of the desert sun.

After leaving Benghazi, we had a relatively smooth and uneventful trip across the Mediterranean to the Lipari Islands. It would have been entirely so if there hadn't been a spot of bother down aft when a couple of the seamen fell out, in a somewhat spectacular way, with one of the engine room staff, which resulted in their becoming the recipients of rather bloody noses. Such an event at sea was almost unheard of despite the often trying conditions they had to put up with, with multi-occupancy cabins being the order of the day for all crew members apart from the petty officers. Needless to say, the troublemakers were duly carpeted, loss of overtime working was their punishment. That may seem a small price to pay for bad behaviour but when earnings at that time were not all that high, a crew member often relied on his overtime payments to ensure his family back home had enough to live on. An offender also risked a logging if there was a repetition of his misdemeanours, which could seriously impair his chances of ongoing employment and end up being almost as painful as a flogging.

'Paul, what's making everybody so bloody withdrawn on this ship?' complained the Fourth Engineer as I took over from him on the last afternoon watch before we arrived at the Lipari Islands.

'I'm no psychologist, Len, but it seems to me that both the Chief and the Second Engineer prefer to live like recluses for reasons best known to themselves. The Second Mate is the liveliest spark amongst the deck crowd. We often share an hour's chat after watch and have a good laugh. But what about the Third Mate? I've hardly spoken to him since I've been on the vessel.'

'Haven't much time for him. He's got ideas bigger than his station. He thinks he's God's gift to women. To hear him talk, women can't wait to be asked out by him.'

29

'That, coming from you, Len, is a bit rich. Sounds like a bit of professional jealousy to me.'

'Right, we shall see. I'll show the bugger the way, you mark my word.'

Quite where the Fourth Engineer was going to perform his promised feats of fatalism, I didn't know. After all, our only other port of call was Messina, for bunkers which required his total involvement. So, if he was going to be as good as his word, the action would have to take place in the Lipari Islands.

Instead of anchoring as we usually did on arrival, we moored alongside a jetty right at the foot of the pumice mountain and it was proposed the pilot launch would help convey our passengers ashore. It was quite feasible to walk the length of the jetty to get ashore, so it looked as if fortune was favouring the brave, provided Len didn't object to using his legs.

It came as no surprise that neither the Chief nor the Second Engineer had any intention of venturing ashore. But this did not mean that I was to be let off my duty night on board, therefore the Fourth made his way ashore alone at the first opportunity possible.

'I saw the Fourth Engineer speeding ashore a short while ago. Let's hope he doesn't bump into the Third Mate on his travels,' remarked the Second Mate.

'Let's hope neither of them get caught up with ,the passengers, Dave. Len is not the most subtle of human beings. If asked whose company he's enjoying, his choice of words to describe the female in question would certainly not be repeatable in mixed company and probably leave the enquirer dumbstruck.'

'I've never managed to get ashore here. Is there much of a town? Lots of shops and entertainment?'

'I haven't a clue because I haven't been ashore myself either. No doubt we'll be fully advised tomorrow by the intrepid adventurers. I don't think they'll find their task easy but you never know their luck. I can tell you this for what it's worth: if his companion is impressed by a no-nonsense approach, then he'll no doubt score a direct hit.'

What actually happened ashore that day depends very much on whose story was to be believed. According to Len, he was strolling along the beach when this bikini-clad surf rider swept ashore, nearly sending him cartwheeling off his feet. It transpired that she was from Germany and on holiday with a party of under 25s. True to form, our Len was not slow to seize the advantage.

By a remarkable coincidence, the Third Mate had met a girl in a bistro who also turned out to be from the same party. She, like Len's new girlfriend, invited him to join their party for an evening get-together in the town centre.

It is highly likely that if either had known they would soon be meeting under the same roof, they would not have ventured forth. According to one of our more mature passengers who claimed he had remained as sober as a judge throughout the evening, the Third Mate had arrived first with his girl-friend but hadn't noticed either him or two of the other passengers from our vessel. They were soon joined by others obviously of German origin, judging by what they were saying. Then finally, in walked Len together with his girlfriend.

To their German hosts, the fact that two of our ship's officers had bumped into each other purely by chance was no big deal. The fact that they did not exactly see eye to eye with one another was not even likely to enter their minds. But as the evening wore on, our passenger friend swore blind it was beginning to dawn on their hosts that their two guests were only concerned in trying to outdo each other, hoping to suitably impress their respective girlfriends.

What neither of them had apparently begun to realise was that the two girls in question seemed more interested in swapping partners. After a fair degree of manoeuvring by the girls, the four of them eventually ended up around the same table. From this moment on, our passenger friend was left with only facial expressions to judge the ongoing events. According to the Third Mate's story, he was going great guns until the arrival on the scene of the Fourth Engineer. He reckoned Len's abrupt, blunt approach had not helped his situation at all. If one believed Len, then the Third Mate's attitude to him put his girlfriend off completely. Having been in the company of the Fourth on several social occasions, I had to agree with our passenger friend that his direct approach to the opposite sex was not always ideal. The consensus of opinion was that far from blaming each other for their singular lack of success, the Third Mate and Fourth Engineer were their own worst enemies.

They were still not talking to one another even by the time we sailed from Messina, but their exploits in the Lipari Islands at least provided a good talking point on the homeward passage to London.

7

On our arrival in London, we were greeted with the news that there were no reliefs for us, which meant, of course, we would not be returning home this time. For myself, this was not a disaster by any manner of means. Provided I could get away to Kent overnight once or twice, I was not all that concerned.

Our Chief Engineer was similarly losing no sleep because of this news as his home was near Rochester and he could easily commute each day to London by train. The Deck Officers were by far the hardest hit although the Captain and Mate were almost resigned to the inevitability of the situation. The Second Mate's wife, however, was determined not to be deprived of her just deserts and was onboard almost before the mooring ropes were secured.

It was suggested we should enjoy an evening's entertainment at the famous Isle of Dogs pub which specialised in female impersonators that brought carloads of patrons down from the West End. Word had spread like wildfire about the value for money that could be obtained in this establishment. The acts that appeared were outrageous both in presentation and content but scored an instant hit with those present. Danny La Rue was already well established as a female impersonator but even he would probably have been slow-handclapped in the presence of some of the speciality acts that appeared at this venue.

The comedy offered was frequently based on parts below the belt, so to speak; but having said that, the laughter and tears in the audience were due to the exquisitely timed double entendres that issued forth at amazingly rapid intervals from the stars who graced the stage.

Sometimes the number of cars trying to park in the vicinity almost blocked the road, and these cars had to be seen to be believed: Bentleys, Porsches, Ferraris, Rolls Royces, just to name a few. We had chosen a good night, for the two 'ladies' on stage were determined to generate maximum laughter from minimum effort. The focus of their attention was, as usual, the parts that certain famous drinks always unfortunately reach and their disapproval of the resulting lack of action. But their ideas for overcoming this frustrating situation had the patrons rolling in the aisles.

'I wonder who writes their scripts,' the Mate exclaimed. 'It's a pity that some of the skill that comes over can't find its way into television. After all, they don't resort to bad language, now do they?'

'No, you're quite right. Their success is based purely on knowing what makes most people laugh and good timing,' I replied.

Just before we sailed on our next voyage, the media were talking about the trouble on the docks. This involved a group of militant London dockers whose sole objective appeared to be the destruction of their own industry, or at least that's how it seemed to many people concerned with shipping. It seemed that no one had explained to these dockers they just didn't have the right to hold the country to ransom in order to pursue their objectives. The media conveniently forgot the trouble the rest of us had to put up with arising from the selfish actions of only a handful of real zealots. There was scarcely a mention of the delayed sailings, cancelled departures, diversions to other ports and the rest of it.

So as we sailed from London, we were left pondering whether we would be returning to this port and, if so, for how long.

Our passengers included a family with a famous soft

drinks background and a daughter whose frivolity created a tremendous atmosphere in the bar but did nothing to calm down her father's shattered nerves. Whether it was the risk of being rejected or simply a little common sense prevailing, I couldn't guess, but neither the Third Mate or the Fourth Engineer attempted any devious tactics to try and trap this girl into their respective lairs.

Then out of the blue, on the day that we steamed past Gibraltar into the Mediterranean, I felt a tap on my shoulder as I sunned myself on the boat deck. Opening my eyes a trifle in the glaring sunlight, I found myself staring up into the eyes of the girl in a million, at least moneywise.

'Hi there, don't you chaps have it easy,' she exclaimed in a soft, refined and elegant tone. 'Do they pay you as well,' she added for good measure.

'Very much so,' I countered. 'We're almost millionaires in a year or so, you know.'

I'd tried to make a genuinely humorous response but the tone of my voice, having just been awakened from the dead, had not struck the right note.

'I see,' she continued unabated. 'Tell me, please, are you all banned from speaking to the passengers? Apart from the Captain and the catering staff, nobody else has spoken to me from the ship's staff.'

I sat up. This was no good at all. It was obvious from the tone of her voice that the poor lass was not enjoying herself one bit and must have wished she had stayed at home. Hardly a wonderful image for the company to live with.

'Look, as you've probably gathered, I'm the Third Engineer. Paul's my name. To answer your question first, there is certainly no ban that prevents us from speaking to passengers but we're a bit wary of saying the wrong thing and ending up getting ourselves into hot water, so to speak.'

'Well, at least that's a start, I'm Lucy and I would love to know where the hot water is.'

I doubled up with laughter. What a character she was. No wonder her father was a nervous wreck.

35

'I'll have a word with the other officers and see if we can get a party organised either at Benghazi or at Malta. OK?'

'That sounds a bit more promising. But what happens in the meantime?'

'I could make several suggestions to help you fill in your time but none of them are all that exciting, I'm afraid. I'd love to invite you down to my cabin but that is playing with fire. Knowing my luck, I'd end up with not only with my colours nailed to the mast but me inside them.'

'My father said that I mustn't miss this trip otherwise I'd never stop complaining about what I'd missed. He says I'm not patient enough but, quite frankly, Paul, I've had more fun in the school playground.'

I had extremely mixed feelings about this girl. She lived in a different world ashore to anything I'd ever experienced and was certainly no innocent cherub. Yet her personality was quite captivating, with a marvellous sense of humour to boot. I had a feeling that some lucky guy in the future would't be sorry he'd found her for himself.

'I've just noticed the time, Lucy. I'm due on watch shortly so I'll have to excuse myself right now. I'll see you later, if you like, before dinner.'

'You had better come up with something, otherwise I shall jump over the side.'

I carefully pondered the situation during my watch. It seemed that the only excitement that might not get any of the participating parties in trouble was a spot of gambling. I remembered our casino when I was Fourth Engineer on the same vessel, but unfortunately the roulette wheel had long since vanished.

There was nothing that I could do directly to put the plan in action because my watchkeeping hours were not conducive to socialising during the evenings whilst at sea. I decided that only the Chief Steward and Stewardess were in a position to implement it, although they would both probably plead that they were too occupied with their routine duties to take on the provision of extra entertainment for the passengers.

'For heaven's sake, Paul, she's just a spoilt young brat who wants everything her own way. I'm certainly not organising anything special for her, entertainment-wise. One of the other passengers has offered to run a poker school, so if she wants to join in, that's fine by me,' commented the Chief Steward when I raised the matter.

8

It wasn't until we had berthed in Benghazi that I bumped into Lucy again.

'What ever happened to you, Paul? You didn't turn up before dinner the other day.'

'We had a spot of trouble to sort out down below and I didn't leave the engine room until just before dinner, so I had my meal in the mess room instead. I wasn't trying to avoid you.'

'Excuse accepted. Now tell me about this party you are supposed to be planning please.'

'Well, I've had a word with the others, and they think it would be best if we leave it until we reach Malta. The dockers work odd hours here and it's hard to get everyone together at the same time. I tell you what, we can probably have a night ashore in Valletta. You'd enjoy a visit to the "Gut", I'm sure,' I added.

I had certainly aroused her curiosity. She had definitely not heard of the downtown street and bars famous to seamen the world over.

'Sounds fascinating. OK, I'll settle for that. Anyway, I'm popping ashore with my folks for the day. Digging sand-castles, more than probably. Wish me luck,' she grimaced.

'There's some pretty good shops in town, Lucy, and if you fancy a flutter, there's always the casino at the Hotel Berenice. Have a good day.'

*

Once again we were faced with the usual dilemma. How long were we going to remain at Benghazi? Would it be possible to carry out essential maintenance work down below or would we be thwarted due to lack of time?

'Second, what do you want me to do? Risk it and tackle the engine valve gear or play safe and do some pump work with the Fourth? There's some electrical jobs that want attending to but I usually do those off watch, as you know.'

'The Chief is insisting that we must keep up with the maintenance on the engines, so you'd better get on with the valve gear, I guess, Third.'

I toiled long and hard with the engine room staff in the sweltering summer heat of the North Africa coast. The physical and mental effort required to maintain such a schedule has to be experienced to be believed. Then, just to add a little more pressure, the Chief Engineer appeared on the plates.

'Are you nearly finished, Third? The Captain has just told me he wants to sail as soon as possible after completion of cargo discharge this afternoon.'

'You must be joking, Chief. The Mate told me this morning that we wouldn't be sailing until mid-morning tomorrow at the earliest.'

'Sorry, Third, it has all changed, once again. Can you say, right now, when you can have the job boxed up for?'

'Bloody hell, Chief, what a sodding waste of time and effort. I'm totally fed up with the way this vessel operates. Anyway, to answer your question, provided we don't have any misfortune and all goes to plan, I would say we'll be finished by about eighteen hundred hours.'

'Right. OK Third, I'll let them know up topsides. You will get there. Keep at it.'

After a day of hard labour, toil and effort, I had the joyous thought of a midnight watch to look forward to. At least I was excused my usual stand by for sailing and, as we sped out of the harbour on schedule, I let the cool spray from the shower jet cascade off my perspiring body and blessed our good fortune in finishing the work on time. All

I needed now was an ice-cold pint shandy, a large scampi salad with French fries and my bunk, strictly in that order.

A sudden deterioration in the weather conditions occurred on passage to Valletta, which meant that we were forced to reduce speed and our arrival slipped back. We didn't berth until late afternoon on my watch instead of in the morning.

'Looks as if we're going to get an extra night here, arriving so late,' suggested the Second Mate.

'I'll believe that when it happens. After the debacle at Benghazi, I'm taking no chances here, whether the Chief likes it or not. Anyway, changing subjects, are we going to have this party and entertain our Lucy or not?'

'You must be joking. Anything to do with that girl is like playing with dynamite. Give her half a chance and she'll end up getting you locked up or joining you in the slammer. Her father leaves you in no doubt about the punishment he'd mete out if you messed up his darling daughter.'

'For heaven's sake, Dave. She's all right provided she gets her own way. You could well be right about her father but I imagine most fathers think the same way about their daughters. Anyway, I might try and get the Fourth Engineer and the Third Mate to join in and we can all introduce her to the "Gut" – provided the Second Engineer will volunteer for night on board duty.'

'Sooner you than me. Don't say I didn't warn you.'

After the close shave in Benghazi, the Chief Engineer didn't push for any main engine overhaul work, just some straightforward routine maintenance, which was a welcome relief.

I had only just got showered and changed when there was a knock on my cabin door.

'It's only me, Lucy.'

I opened my door. 'Hello there, had a good day ashore?'

'I suppose so, if you call that traipsing around churches,

ruins and hot dusty streets accompanied by non-stop bells and a few too many smells for my liking. Am I allowed to enter your lair?'

'You'll get me shot, but I guess I'll survive.'

She accepted a cold beer and then wasted no time in finding out what was planned for her at Malta.

'Three of us are going down to the "Gut" tonight. I'm not at all sure that your parents would approve, but if they're OK about it, you're very welcome to join us. We'll make sure you get back in one piece. We don't think a party on board has a cat in hell's chance of being a great success.'

'Right, that's fine by me, Paul. What time are we going? Can't wait to get there.'

'Heh, wait a minute. We can't take you if your folks are against the idea. You might not like the bars and atmosphere, anyway. You'll have to put up with lots of suggestive remarks, at the very least.'

'You don't know my folks like I do. They'll be all right about it, I know.'

My problem was that I just hadn't had time to mention the idea to the other parties and time was running out fast.

'It's the Fourth's turn for night on board duty. I'm going ashore myself tonight, Third,' the Second Engineer told me. 'I doubt if the Chief will cover for him but you can give him a try if you like.'

I had no intention of asking the Chief. We would never hear the end of it if he had an emergency crop up while we were all ashore.

That left the Third Mate. I just hoped he wouldn't scupper my plan or Lucy would never forgive me either.

'I suppose so, Paul. I can't say she's my kind of dame, but if it will keep you happy, I'll suffer along with you.'

The relief was more than welcome. Fortunately for us, there were no naval vessels in port, which at least gave us a fighting chance of surviving the evening with some degree

41

of credibility. Even so, I was wondering what the bar girls would make of Lucy and she of them.

We were sitting in a bar almost half-way down the "Gut". Lucy was taking it all well in her stride, giving every indication that she felt quite at home.

'At last I can relax and let go. Are these girls on the game?'

She was referring to the crowd of females who are always hanging around the bars in the 'Gut'.

'If they were, they wouldn't last very long in these establishments. They are here solely to increase the bar turnover and profits. They persuade us to buy them a drink and what they get served is coloured water, but of course we muggins are charged for pricey cocktails. Goodness knows what they get paid by the bar owners for ripping us off.'

Then, almost as if to drive the point home, two of the girls made for our table, complete with stools, and sat beside the Third Mate and myself, not even sparing a glance for poor Lucy.

'Hi, sailor boy, you want plenty fun with me?'

'No, not tonight, thanks, honeypot,' I replied.

The Third Mate similarly turned down the other girl's offer.

'You hurt my feelings, lover boy. Now I need a drink to make me feel better. OK.'

Before I could answer, she'd waved over the barman who appeared in a flash with two drinks on his tray for our two 'guests' and demanded prompt payment. Even before he had been paid, they had finished their drinks and were on their feet.

'Maybe you come back tomorrow night and we have more fun,' she suggested.

'Not if I can help it, dream girl,' I replied.

With that, they were gone.

'My, my,' said Lucy, 'I think I've found a new market for my father's firm's drinks. It's a guaranteed winner.'

42

'Not really, Lucy,' the Third Mate added. 'If these girls are prepared to drink coloured water. I don't think the bars will be stocking up with anything of real value.'

At least Lucy was grateful for our efforts to entertain her, and after we delivered her safely back on board, she thanked us profusely for the experience.

9

It was no surprise that our stay at Valletta was interrupted by frequent shift of berths, and finally we anchored at buoys in the harbour where we loaded seed potatoes for the UK. There was no further opportunity to stretch our legs ashore and I just hoped that despite the limited maintenance we had managed to accomplish during the voyage, we would not experience any major problems and remain on schedule. I had a particular interest in arriving back in London at our expected time because of the christening of my sister's daughter in Kent.

Our passage to Ceuta passed without incident and, after bunkering, we continued our voyage back to London. Once again, we had only a little cargo on board and were therefore grateful that the weather was relatively calm, particularly through the Bay of Biscay, with the vessel riding in a reasonably comfortable manner in the swell. We maintained a good speed, reaching London on our ETA, to be met with the news that because of the current unrest in the docks with strike threats almost daily, the company required us to remain on board with no reliefs provided.

It did not take a special investigator to work out that the situation in the docks was worsening on an almost daily basis. There seemed no end to the demands of the stevedores union, with other unions and work-forces being actively encouraged to join in the free-for-all. The anger that we seafarers felt in not only personally being hijacked, but seeing the mischief that was being caused to our families and to the nation as a whole, could never have been imagined by the perpetrators. It remained to be seen whether the Port of London could withstand the onslaught of its own dock working force but many of us were highly sceptical. Of one thing there was no doubt at all: if the country was going to progress, there was going to have to be a radical rethink with regard to industrial relations and a vast improvement in managerial skills and production practices. Otherwise, we were all heading for the slippery slope.

Only the Chief Engineer was able to get home of an evening. The rest of us had to suffer in silence, and my girlfriend in Kent was convinced that I was working for totally unreasonable employers who gave personal matters no consideration at all when it came to their seafaring staff.

That was a thought also currently passing through my sister's mind. She appreciated my frustration and disappointment at being defeated by circumstances beyond my control but I still had a tense time explaining to them both that, on this occasion, the company itself was a victim of circumstances beyond its control as well.

Our only relief from the daily routine on board was to escape to the local pubs for a nightly noggin or two, so the news that we were going to sail as scheduled, regardless of the cargo loaded, was more than welcome and at least cocked a snoop at our tormentors.

Another surprise in store was the unusual fact that all of our passengers on the forthcoming voyage were known to each other. They had simply made a block booking well in advance of the sailing date. No doubt the Chief Steward would be hoping for record bar sales, but that would depend on what their idea of enjoyment amounted to. After all, a block booking by members of the Temperance Society would hardly do anything to improve his takings.

As it turned out, both the Chief Steward and ourselves were very fortunate in having a party of workers and their wives from a small firm in Sussex. There was no doubt whatsoever, they were determined not to waste any time in getting the bar opened for business, as I quite unintentionally found out shortly after they had boarded.

'Officer, how do you get a bloody drink on this fine ship? I'm nearly passing out,' chirped a smiling, perspiring, somewhat overweight but charming middle-aged gentleman, dressed more appropriately for a seminar than a holiday.

'I'm afraid that's not my department but I will put in a request on your behalf. The bar doesn't usually open on sailing day until our departure time but I'll see what I can do. No promises, though,' I replied.

For once, I struck a responsive note with the catering department and the stewardess volunteered to serve drinks in the passenger lounge although the bar had to remain closed until departure time.

I soon realised that we were luckier than normal with our passengers, who were certainly not going to let a bit of bad weather in the Bay of Biscay spoil their great adventure. Amazingly enough, they appeared with great gusto for their meals, which they insisted be accompanied at all times by suitable vintage wine. We were somewhat taken back by their enthusiasm generally, with the Chief Steward showing signs of very mixed feelings about his brood. Of course, his bar takings were heading for record profits, but debating whether he would have to make further purchases of food abroad to keep up with their insatiable hunger was obviously causing him a great deal of stress. After all, he had to think about his personal bank balance, and it would be relatively unheard of for a chief steward to be on the losing side when it came to reckoning up the catering costs for the voyage.

Once again, we bunkered at Ceuta before entering the Mediterranean and then continued on towards Benghazi. The weather was simply superb for early November and during the middle of my afternoon watch, the Chief Engineer telephoned me to ask if I would mind showing a few of the passengers around the engine and boiler rooms. This was nothing new, and usually there were two or no more than three of them to cope with at any one time. Imagine my surprise on greeting them at the entrance door to find them trooping in one after another, with the Chief bringing up the rear. I had no chance to warn the other watch personnel of this unusual influx and there were some stares of amazement. Despite the heat and humidity, they all completed the full tour unscathed but were obviously very relieved to be heading out again into the fresh air on deck.

After I had completed my watch and before diving into the shower, I took a quick breath of fresh air on the after deck. A voice called down from the boat deck above, 'I just don't know how you can put up with the temperature down there in the engine room for up to four hours. Half an hour was more than enough for me. They just don't know how lucky they are up there.'

The voice belonged to the gentleman whose thirst I had helped to slake before we left London and, as he uttered his final words, he pointed very clearly up to the bridge.

'To be honest, in the middle of summer, it's even hotter, and I don't think the Chief would have agreed to a visit if it had been then. But to answer your question, the main thing that keeps one going is the sheer luxury of escaping for eight hours from the heat, if you're lucky, cold showers, iced drinks and, usually, very good food. They may have it relatively easy most of the time but there are occasions when most engineers wouldn't wish to change places with a deck officer, bad weather and fog being just two.'

It had somehow come to the passenger's attention that we often paid a visit to the NAAFI at Benghazi and it took a good deal of gentle persuasion by the stewardess to make them forget their idea of joining us. I suggested they visit the local casino instead and promised to join them, provided I could slip away from the NAAFI.

It looked as if we were only going to have a couple of days in Benghazi but the Chief was adamant that we tackle work on the main engines. So, following an early morning arrival and four hours' rest, it was back to the grindstone. By the time the day's labours had been completed, I was not feeling all that enthusiastic about either a visit to the NAAFI or the casino later.

Once again, though the call of the shore drowned out the doubts. Our friends at the NAAFI had got wind of our arrival and had laid on not just a buffet but also a few dancing girls to entertain us. I felt quite guilty at leaving prematurely but did not want to break my promise to the passengers.

I always had a feeling of being very much the poor relation when I entered the casino at the Hotel Berenice. After all, oil-rich millionaires, business leaders, shop owners and their entourages frequented the gaming hall and there was no way that I could afford to join in their fun.

I didn't notice our passengers at first but then spotted them surrounding one of the roulette wheels. Their attention was so directed on the immediate events that were happening in front of their very eyes that they didn't notice my arrival on the scene. I placed a straight red or black number bet. It proved to be a winner but at odds of only 2 to 1 it hardly made me an overnight millionaire. But it did have the desired result.

'Well, I'd be blowed. It's the Third Engineer showing us how to be a winner,' announced the wife of the party leader.

'I only wish I had a truly winning formula. I'd be quite happy to share it with you,' I replied. 'When we had our own roulette wheel on the ship, I spun the wheel for hours on end trying to work out the odds of any particular number repeating itself but it was all in vain. One thing you can be sure of, the chances of the bank losing out on roulette are extremely remote.'

Then just as if to demonstrate I was talking a lot of rubbish, the lady's husband pulled off a single-number win. The temptation was to try and repeat the win and throw the winnings away on a forlorn hope. This time the winner decided to call it a day whilst in profit and promptly treated us to drinks all round.

It certainly had been a night to remember for our lucky passenger.

10

During our voyage from Benghazi to Messina, problems started to develop with our main engine governor, a piece of equipment that was designed to prevent the engines from over-speeding. This was not a major headache, provided we were able to maintain the exhaust steam turbine in operation, as this piece of machinery was also quite capable of preventing any engine over-speeding. Then, just to add to our difficulties, we were told that our intended stay at Messina would be just for one day as there was little cargo to handle.

Apart from the disappointment for the passengers, there just wasn't sufficient time to carry out suitable repairs to the governor, so once again, it would be a case of pressing on regardless to the Lipari Islands to load our usual cargo before commencing the return voyage to London.

Despite the Chief Engineer's attempts to persuade the powers that be to arrange for the vessel to berth alongside at the Lipari Islands so that we could deal with repairs in an adequate manner, we ended up, as usual, anchored with no chance to put matters right. After completion of loading, we were under way, bound for London.

Our passage westbound towards Gibraltar proved to be smooth enough for even the most susceptible person, but as soon as we headed out into the Atlantic Ocean, the weather deteriorated. Even so, we made reasonable progress, passing Cape St Vincent on schedule, but after passing Lisbon, gale force winds made their presence very much felt. This weather persisted right into the Bay of Biscay. The vessel began to roll heavily in significant beam seas as I appeared in the engine room for my afternoon watch. We were by no means loaded to our usual draft and, having consumed a fair amount of both fuel and fresh water since leaving Messina, we were even more prone to the heavy weather. My concern, though, wasn't simply trying to prevent myself being wrong-footed by the vessel's excessive rolling movements. On monitoring the engine instrumentation, it soon became apparent that our main cooling water system for the condenser was not performing correctly for one very simple reason. Due to the extent of the rolling, the main sea cooling water low intake on the port side was unbelievably being uncovered and the circulating pump was losing its suction because of drawing air. As if that wasn't enough, the engine speed governor reminded us of our lack of opportunity to rectify its deficiencies, with the engines trying to race away at a disconcerting speed.

'Look, Fourth, we can't go on like this. As soon as you go off watch, explain what's going on down here to the Chief and tell him that I need to reduce our engine speed, otherwise we're going to be in big trouble. He'll have to get the Old Man's agreement. OK?'

The Fourth acknowledged the reason for my request with considerable concern and disappeared up topsides, like a rabbit into a bolthole.

A short while passed and I'd heard nothing about reducing speed.

'This is just bloody ludicrous,' I exclaimed to my watch rating as the vessel once again commenced a series of massive rolling movements. 'I'm going to ring the bridge and request a speed reduction.'

I might as well have asked for a trip to the moon, such was the response. Didn't I appreciate how important it was to maintain our speed lest the bad weather delay our arrival in London? The technical problems were no concern of the bridge. Wasn't that the purpose of carrying engineers on vessels?

Before I could respond to the bridge, the vessel rolled

violently to port and almost simultaneously the exhaust turbine governor operated and the main engines, released from all speed control, almost took off despite my belated attempts to stop them by closing the main control valve.

'What the hell,' I shouted across the engine room to the watch rating.

What sounded like a series of cannons firing rent the engine room and I stared in amazement at the shocked expression of the watchkeeper, who obviously couldn't believe what he had just witnessed. That was enough reason for me to ring the telegraph to slow ahead and reduce the engine speed further before I sped round to the other side of the engine room to see for myself just how bad the news really was.

At least, that was my intention but before I could set off, the bells were ringing, certainly for me, not my girl. I grabbed the bridge phone.

'Before you say anything, we have an emergency in the engine room. I'll let you know how serious it is as soon as I've had chance to investigate. In the meantime, I'll try and keep the main engines running but I can't guarantee that.' With that I replaced the telephone and rushed to the scene of misfortune. I couldn't believe my eyes either. The outer casing of the main air pump had shattered and was fractured around almost the full circumference. Only a small inspection plate was holding the halves together. Feed water was pouring into the bilges instead of being returned to the boilers. I was quickly joined by the off watch engineers and the Chief.

'We can't stop the engines in this weather, can we, Chief, otherwise we'll lose the vessel', I pleaded.

'Right, Third, keep your head. See if there's anything we can do in the way of a temporary repair while the engines are running. I'm going straight up to the Old Man to see if we can get some assistance, that is, if there are any ships in the vicinity.' With that the Chief was gone.

The main air pump was no small piece of equipment, being about 2 metres in diameter and almost as high. It was operated by two long levers connected to the high pressure engine assembly.

It soon became obvious that the engine room bilges were filling up with water faster than the pumps could cope and with the violent rolling we were experiencing, bilge water was rushing up the ship's sides to the first platform level. Unless we took action quickly, our generators, located at the lower level, would soon be well and truly out of action.

Looking back at this mind-bending situation, it was probably the sight of all that water in the wrong place that galvanised the Fourth Engineer and myself into action. We just had to get those shattered halves of the air pump brought back together again as soon as possible. We also had to get some water into the boilers before it was too late. Even more importantly, the bilges had to be pumped out quickly otherwise we were goners for sure.

'Len, what we need to do is to try and fit strongbacks underneath and across the top of the air pump. We'll need some long screwed rods to join these together then we might be able to draw the air pump back together again.' Easier said than done but, in the situation we were faced with, a job that simply had to be achieved.

Then the Fourth Engineer had a flash of inspiration.

'I know there's nothing suitable in our stores to make the strongbacks but the hatch top bars that hold down the covers would do.'

'Right, see the Mate, he might have a spare bar available that we can cut up. Air tube stopper rods should be long enough to use to join the strongbacks together. We've plenty of them, I know. While you're trying to get your hands on a hatch bar, I've got to do something about these bilges. The water has nearly reached plate level.'

The Chief Engineer had returned to the engine room and, with the Second Engineer, was desperately trying to keep the main steam plant operating with ever diminishing boiler water levels and ever increasing bilge levels.

'Chief, the bilge pipes and strums must be choked,' I shouted.

'I know,' answered the Chief. 'But if we use the main circulating pump and the direct bilge injection, we risk choking up the main condenser, then all will be lost.'

'We'll have to try the portable emergency pipes and connect them to the main ballast pump on overboard discharge,' I volunteered.

'I doubt if that will be enough.' By then, though, the Chief was willing to try anything to relieve our ever worsening situation.

The only snag was that the emergency bilge pipes were stored at the wrong end of the propeller shaft tunnel, which by then was half full of water.

Naturally enough, there were no volunteers to proceed along the tunnel so, grabbing the nearest tools to hand, I waded down. My attempts to release the clips holding the pipes in position were despairingly frustrated by seizure of the nuts securing the clips. It looked as if the pipes hadn't been removed and used for years. Only a hammer and chisel would do the job now. I struggled back along the tunnel to the engine room.

'For God's sake, get me a large hammer and a sharp chisel,' I gasped at a rating who was clinging to the guard rails around the turbine plant. 'Move yourself, man or we'll all be goners.'

He got the message and shot off to the stores.

Once again, with the required tools, I entered the tunnel for what would be the last time if I wasn't successful in removing the pipes. I reckoned that I had five minutes at the most to accomplish the task.

It's amazing what can be achieved in desperate circumstances. The pipes almost leaping off the bulkhead as I chiselled off the wretched nuts. All I could do now was float them along the tunnel, then couple them up to one another and finally to the main ballast pump. I dropped the free end into the bilges.

'Right,' I said to one of the ratings, 'make sure that strum filter doesn't choke up.'

I started the pump and hoped for the best.

'Here you are, Third.' I was handed a mug of tea by the Donkeyman.

'Bless you, Donks, very welcome indeed.'

I rested for a few minutes, wondering just how much longer the engines could be left running before we repaired the broken air pump.

'I think we're winning with the bilges.' The Chief had also grabbed a mug of tea and was looking a little less stressed. 'Incidentally, the Old Man has been down to tell me a Mayday has been transmitted but apparently there isn't another vessel within five hundred miles of us.'

The Fourth Engineer suddenly re-appeared in the engine room. He was absolutely sodden.

'What the hell have you been doing, Len,' I said.

'Well, the Mate told me to help myself to a hatch bar in use because he has no spares. The Third Mate helped me to remove one. What a bloody job, we nearly got washed overboard.'

'That wasn't very clever, but as you got it, we'd better use it quick before it's too late,' I replied.

I explained quickly to the Fourth Engineer what we needed to do with the materials we had available.

'You must be joking, Paul. Can you see us sawing through this bar and drilling the holes in this weather.'

'Look, if you can get out on deck in this weather, remove a bar and get it down here, we're going to do whatever's necessary to use it,' I replied.

'OK, we'll take it in turns and the ratings can hang on to us and try to keep us in one place while we perform.

11

If ever there was a time when our guardian angels were so desperately needed, it was right now. It took us nearly an hour to prepare the strongback bars and the tie rods, our nerves and muscles straining to keep us where we needed to be as the vessel's motion tried to throw us onto our backsides. Somehow the broken halves of the pump hung in together as the engines slowly turned. Our only relief was to have stopped the bilge water racing up the ship's sides.

'Tell me, Paul, how the hell are we supposed to fit this gear to the air pump without getting scalded and decapitated, with the engines still turning?'

'You'll have to try and hold one of the bars under the pump while I try and persuade the rods to pass through the holes in the top bar and fasten the nuts. If I can't get the nuts onto the rods in the second or so available, we'll have to ask the Chief to stop the engines briefly then repeat the same thing for the other two bars.'

I couldn't have had a better engineer to work with. Len grimaced as the scalding hot feed water seeped through his boiler suit. I fared no better. We both gasped with the pain but hung on for grim death.

'Watch it Len. You nearly bought it then.'

His head was periously close to the link levers that were coupled to the pump crosshead.

'OK, Len, that's the nuts on the rods. Let's start nipping them up – but slowly, for Pete's sake. We don't want the rods to break.'

We struggled on, hoping against hope that no more disasters would befall us at that time.

'Paul, dare I say it but I think we're winning. Look how little water is leaking from the pump now.'

I had gone on watch and noon and it was now nearly ten p.m. There was just the Chief and the Fourth Engineer, myself and the watch ratings still down below. We had increased the engine speed to half, much to the relief of the Captain.

'I think we ought to try to add a bit more strength to the repair,' suggested the Fourth. 'We don't know how much longer it will last.'

'Len, I've had enough. I'm due back on watch in a couple of hours and I haven't eaten. If you think you can do more without interfering with what we've already done, go ahead by all means. I'm going to grab a sandwich and then hit the hay.'

I climbed wearily up the engine room ladders and made my way to the mess room, in the firm belief that the catering department would have left some food handy, at least sandwiches. Not a bite to be seen and no one from the department around. Marvellous, a cup of tea. What a shambles.

Midnight came and I was back on watch, wondering how things were going.

'Have a look and see what you think,' said the Fourth.

'Yes, that's better,' I replied.

He had strengthened the strongbacks with larger screw rods and heavy steel washers which he had found in the store room. I glanced at the vacuum gauge and was astonished to see that it had increased to a point where it would be safe to engage the exhaust turbine.

'I'm going to ring the bridge and tell them we can increase speed once again,' I informed the Fourth Engineer.

The weather gradually improved, as did our speed, and 18 hours later we berthed in the Millwall Dock at London. Our reception committee included representatives and surveyors from the Department of Transport who were more than a little interested in our emergency repairs. We were feeling quite pleased with ourselves, and their favourable comments helped to boost our spirits no end.

Because of the long time it would take to obtain a replacement air pump and to avoid these delays, the powers that be decided that the broken parts could be mended by metal stitching, a technique well established and accepted by the Classification Societies whose job it is to ensure that vessels are kept up to scratch.

Once again, there were no relief engineers available but the Chief agreed to my taking a few days off down in Kent provided I kept in regular contact with him. We had already decided that if the relief situation didn't improve, we would have to spell each other, otherwise none of us would get a break whilst the vessel was back in the UK.

Shortly after we berthed, and after bidding farewell to our passengers, I was on a tube to Victoria Station to catch a Ramsgate-bound train. The physical and mental stresses and strains of the last few days were by now beginning to make themselves felt, but it wasn't till a dear old lady seated opposite me made a meaningful comment that the penny really dropped.

'Young man, you look as if you have just been through a terrible ordeal. I hope you don't mind my saying so?'

'Not at all,' I replied. 'You're nearer the truth than you could possibly imagine.' I briefly recounted the tale leaving out all the technical details.

'I thought so,' she said. 'Well, I do hope you have a good long rest and put it all behind you.'

'Seeing my sister, family and friends will soon put me in a good frame of mind, but the long rest is still some way off, I'm afraid.'

Once again, I was going to turn up out of the blue at my sister's home, but this was never a problem for her or her husband. They had moved home once again, this time to an idyllic Kent country cottage – or at least that was what it would be by the time they had completed the improvements. The only way to reach the first floor was by means of a builder's ladder. This was a marvellous way of deterring lazy burglars but not to be recommended for anyone with sleepwalking tendencies.

I decided that I should try and show my gratitude for all the hospitality afforded to me and set about carving a car access through a typical country hedgerow so that two cars could park on the land next to the cottage. It would have helped no end if there had been power tools available but I struggled on with my chosen task, and in the course of one back-breaking day an access appeared, to the utter delight of my sister and the amazement of my brother-in-law.

'Paul, are you contacting Christine while you're here? She's always asking for news of your whereabouts. While we really appreciate what you've just accomplished out there, I don't think she will exactly jump over the moon if she thinks you haven't had time to see her because of your labours on our behalf.'

Of course my sister was right.

'I'd better not ring her at work. I'll give her a call early evening and see if she is free,' I replied.

It was late afternoon. I was still outside tidying up when I heard the telephone ring, then my sister called out. 'Paul, it's for you. I think he said he was the Chief.'

'Hello, yes, Chief, it's the Third. What's the matter?'

The Chief did not sound too pleased.

'I'm afraid you'll have to return to London tonight. There's been another development. The insurance people want to talk to all the ship's officers, particularly you. It sounds as if they aren't too happy about what happened. Apart from that, the Superintendent is not too pleased that I let you go as quickly as I did and he wants you back immediately. Sorry, Third.'

'OK, Chief. It's not your fault. I'll get my sister to run me down to Whitstable station. There's a train every hour, as you know, so I should be back on board for about eight p.m.'

12

Not for the first time in my life did I find that being frank and honest was hardly the most rewarding attitude to adopt in dealing with insurance investigators. The fact that I'd done everything humanly possible to avoid a calamity apparently did not count for much in their reckoning. My crime was that I had not personally informed the Chief Engineer of the unusual problems that we were experiencing with the main engines, although the Chief was trying to tell the investigators that he was already aware of the engine governor problem. The downright bad luck of the turbine governor cutting in owing to the engine governor problem combined with the bad weather was apparently an event which I should have predicted, despite the fact that none of us had ever experienced that happening in all our previous seagoing experience.

During a particularly trying question-and-answer session, the company's London-based Senior Superintendent Engineer made an impromptu but timely visit to the vessel. On grasping what was being suggested by the investigators, he directly intervened and didn't mince his words.

'Gentlemen, the Department of Transport are entirely satisfied with the actions taken by the vessel's engineers to get this vessel safely back to port with no injuries or loss of life and no further damage to the machinery or any damage to the vessel, thank God. Your questions should be directed to the Captain. Ask him why he didn't acknowledge the need for a reduction in speed just before the accident or at least question the Chief Engineer about the matter.'

Their reaction was almost as predictable as night following day.

'Thank you for your advice but we do not require your opinion on these matters at the present time. However, rest assured there are a number of answers we shall require from you, not least of all the company's policy about ensuring that urgent maintenance work is carried out when required.'

The Chief beckoned me to leave the passenger lounge. He knew the Superintendent well and did not want me to be a party to what was obviously developing into a heated slanging match.

'Not to worry, Third, worst things happen at sea, now don't they?' was the Chief's rather cryptic comment when I asked afterwards what had transpired after my premature departure from the scene. 'Anyway, it looks as if we're not going to complete repairs until next week, so you can return to your sister's home. Keep in daily contact with me on the telephone just in case there are any more rabbits sprung out of the hat for us, OK?'

I thanked the Chief and caught the train back down to Kent that afternoon, once again receiving a warm welcome.

'Everything sorted out now then?' asked my brother-in-law on his return from work that evening.

'More or less, Charles, but you can never be sure. Our Superintendent got well and truly steamed up about the questioning although I didn't stay to witness his performance in full.'

I gave my girlfriend Christine a ring but was disappointed to find out that she was having to babysit at home because her mother was going out.

'Paul, you know where we live. Why don't you come round? It would be lovely to see you. My mum won't mind in the least, I know.'

'If you're sure. I'll drive over after tea. Look forward to seeing you.'

*

Despite the time that had elapsed since we had last seen each other, a feeling of instant rapport soon emerged, but it was equally as clear that her younger sister was not going to be left out of the act. After all, she was not going to bed until she had heard all about my adventures, even though they could hardly be deemed the Enid Blyton type.

Fortunately, a combination of her tiredness and my inability as a raconteur soon ensured ever deeper yawns and slumber. The two of us managed to carry her up to bed and after duly tucking her in, and with the obligatory kiss we crept out of her room.

'I can't offer you much choice drinkwise, Paul. I'm afraid we need restocking in the alcohol department. There's a drop of gin, a bit more sherry and plenty of coffee.'

'No problem. A coffee would be fine, thanks.'

She returned shortly afterwards, with just one cup of coffee.

'Aren't you having one?' I enquired.

'Paul, would you mind if I excuse myself for a short while? I promised myself a bath once I got home from work. I don't think there's much on television but you're welcome to try out the music centre. There's stacks of records to choose from.'

'Sure, you go ahead. But what shall I do if the phone rings while you're in the bath?'

'Well, you can't leave it ringing otherwise you know who will wake up. Just say you're my boyfriend and that we'll get back.'

I settled down to enjoy my coffee and listen to a selection of Burt Bacharach songs. Fortunately the telephone didn't ring, but after a while it suddenly dawned on me that the tapping I thought was part of the rhythm accompaniment to the music was actually coming from the ceiling above. Thinking it was the younger sister up to her tricks, I crept up the stairs and opened her bedroom door quietly, to find her sound asleep.

'Is that you, Paul?' Christine whispered. 'I need my back scrubbing, if you don't mind.'

I moved down the landing to the bathroom door.

'Was that you tapping on the floor? I thought it was your sister.'

'Of course it was me. Are you OK?'

'Yes, I'm fine. Just a little surprised. I don't get invited into my girlfriends' bathrooms every day of the week. Your mum isn't likely to return in the next half-hour or so, I hope.'

'No, of course not, you blithering idiot. My mum won't be back until the early hours, that I do know.'

I suppose I loved to live dangerously, at least when it came to the fairer sex. Any thoughts of getting carried away, though, were firmly kept in place by the possibility of quickly having to abandon ship, so to speak, if her sister decided to try sleepwalking or, worse still, wake up and report the facts to her dear mum.

In any event, my natural feelings were rapidly overtaking my caution, so I entered and did as bid.

Next day, when asked by my sister, how the babysitting had gone, I was able to say with all honesty that it had been a very enlightening experience.

Christine worked in Canterbury as a secretary and I'd arranged to meet her during her lunch hour.

'How's my lover boy, then?' I was greeted with, accompanied by a fit of the giggles.

'Chance would be a fine thing,' I replied, adding, 'Mind you, the scenery was absolutely fabulous.'

That comment at least earned me an enormous hug and kiss, much to my embarrassment, in the middle of the pavement right outside the main post office in full view of the midday crowd of office workers and tourists.

'I just wish you didn't have to keep disappearing off the scene, Paul. It seems we hardly have time to see one another before you're on your way to some distant land.'

'I know how you feel, but what I'm doing is my career at the present time. If I can pass all the exams and qualify as a chief engineer then this will give me a better chance ashore. I shan't be staying at sea for ever, you know.'

'It's daft really. We hardly know each other and here am I talking as if we were on the point of getting engaged. I'm sorry.'

I could not help thinking that I might have the same problem to face even more frequently in the future.

13

As usual, this stay at my sister's home was once again all too brief. The warmth and generosity of her hospitality contrasted enormously with the often bleak 'home comforts' whilst away at sea. I was dwelling, somewhat absentmindedly, on such thoughts while waiting to leave to catch the train back to London. My sister was taking me in her car to the local railway station, a distance of about 5 miles. I had glanced at my watch several times but only when I checked the clock in her kitchen did I come to my senses with a sickening crunch. My watch had stopped, not just a few minutes ago but nearly half an hour before. My gasp of horror brought my sister rushing into the room.

'Oh, my God, Jennifer, my ruddy watch has stopped. The train is due in fifteen minutes. We haven't a cat in hell's chance of catching it, have we?'

My sister was devastated as she had relied on me to tell her when it was time to leave. She was a very busy person with a young daughter to cope with, apart from doing secretarial work at home. She was also determined to try to beat the clock and the train. We flew through the country lanes at breathtaking speed. I feared the worst. The Chief Engineer's last words to me the night before on the telephone, were ringing in my ears:

'We are definitely sailing at fourteen hundred hours tomorrow, so you must be on board at least an hour before. Don't be late, under any circumstances. Is that clear?'

She couldn't have done more but the train was already leaving the station as we arrived.

'I'll run you up to London in the car, otherwise you're not going to make it in time, are you?'

'No, Jennifer, you're not used to driving in London and with a young child in the back, it could be a nightmare for you. Thanks for the offer all the same, but I'll catch the next train and hope for the best.'

After a lot of protests, my sister acknowledged the situation and reluctantly left. I waited for what seemed an eternity.

At last, I boarded and was moving swiftly in the right direction. I prayed silently for no delays en route. Fortunately there were none and we arrived at Victoria Station more or less on time. I ran as fast as I could to the taxi rank and leapt into a waiting cab.

'Where to, mate?' the cabbie asked.

'West India Dock, as fast as you can. You can name your own price. I shall be in big, big trouble if I'm not there within the next half-hour.'

'Really, what's the big deal?' he asked as we roared off in a manner more appropriate for the starting grid at Brands Hatch.

I quickly explained the terrible situation and left him in no doubt whatsoever about the dire consequences I would have to face if I was late. Whether or not he'd ever driven competitively on a race track I had no idea, but on the day in question he was certainly winning the London Grand Prix. There were a few heart-stopping moments but my cabbie was comfortably in command, glowing in his own performance.

We finally raced onto the dock to the vessel's berth and my heart almost stopped. No ship. My mind raced.

'Where to now, mate?' the cabbie enquired.

'Round to the lock pit. Let's hope it's there.'

It was, waiting to enter the lock.

'I'll never be able to thank you enough. What do I owe you?' I asked.

'Let's say a tenner, mate, OK?'

I gave him £15 and bid him farewell.

'The Captain wants you up topside,' said the Chief as I unlocked my cabin door. 'What the hell happened? You've given us all kittens.'

I quickly briefed the Chief of my misfortune. The Old Man was obviously upset. Surprisingly enough, he accepted the reason I gave him for my belated return. I'd never previously been caught out by such circumstances and my concern obviously showed on my face.

'I'm prepared to accept your apology on this occasion but if you ever find yourself in a similar situation again, heaven forbid, then make sure you contact the vessel's agents so they can let us know. Is that clearly understood, Third?'

'Certainly, but I can assure you, sir, that I'll be purchasing a first-class reliable timepiece as soon as I can. I never want to find myself in that situation again as long as I live.'

The only saving grace, as far as I was concerned, was that I didn't have to face any embarrassing questions from the passengers as we had none on this voyage. It was getting too close to Christmas for those wanting to be at home to run the risk of the vessel not returning to the UK in time for the festivities. Our itinery included several North African ports, Algiers in particular, where time could almost stand still whilst we waited for the required action to take place, therefore we were sceptical about our chances of being back in time.

We were satisfied that the repairs carried out in London to our damaged pump had been accomplished with adequate expertise and we had no more problems with it. The weather, at least, was very much in our favour and we made good progress as far as Algiers. Even fortune favoured us here as there was little shipping in the port and before we had time to ponder our fate, it was time to be on our way again. Then, almost out of the blue, sprang gale force winds and extremely heavy seas, which persisted until our arrival at Benghazi.

Ramadan was very much in force, which, as usual, meant

some delays. We put in our usual appearance at the Army camp and were invited to a party in the sergeants' mess. Our hosts were quite envious that we could be back in the UK for Christmas but this envy didn't show itself in their hospitality. Whilst we were in the midst of the revelry, word reached the camp that there were some problems in the harbour, with the mooring ropes of some of the vessels parting due to the high winds. None of us had realised how much they had increased in force since we had come ashore.

We quickly decided that we should return to our vessel without delay and our hosts immediately provided transport for us back to the harbour.

The sight that met our eyes was quite astonishing. Two vessels had parted their moorings and been blown across the harbour, one alongside our vessel. This had caused our vessel to be shifted along the quay wall, and our gangway was lying in a rather misshapen condition on the quay. Our crew were trying to manhandle the other gangway round to the quay side of the vessel, but in the dreadful conditions this task was proving to be extremely demanding.

In the end, the pilot ladder was rigged and, like monkeys in a forest, we clambered upwards and scrambled on board.

The chief engineer was more than a little relieved to see us safely back.

'The Fourth and myself have prepared for stand by down below. The old man thinks we might have to manoeuvre clear of this berth but the harbour authorities haven't given him any orders yet, so we'll just have to wait and see,' he advised us.

The Second Engineer suggested that I get my head down without further ado. He was going to commence sea-going watches straight away and I could squeeze in a couple of hours shut-eye before turning to once again.

Imagine my surprise when I received the usual call for breakfast, having slept solidly for nigh on ten hours. The harbour authorities had decided to shift us but provided a couple of tugs to do the job, so the sea watches were cancelled.

14

Apart from some damage to the gangway and several parted mooring ropes, we escaped relatively lightly, much to our relief, from what could potentially have been a disastrous incident. Once again, I reckoned our guardian angels had been working overtime to protect us and it was with some sense of relief that we finally sailed from Benghazi. Our passage to Malta was relatively peaceful with only routine duties to have to fulfil. I just hoped we would be berthed at a quay rather than anchored at the buoys which made getting ashore in Valletta harbour not an easy task.

'Third, fancy a trip out of Valletta?' The Second Mate was keen to explore the coastal areas. Apparently, he had promised his wife a holiday in Malta and wanted to find out whether or not the widely publicised hotels were as good as they were cracked up to be.

'How do you propose we carry out this mission, Dave?' I enquired. 'I'm not sure yet what our programme is. The Chief manages to spring a few surprises whenever he can, so I might not be able to get ashore during the day.'

'How about us hiring a car?' he suggested.

'Are you telepathic or do you happen to know that when I last sailed on this ship as Fourth Engineer, I did exactly that. We were supposed to be doing the very thing that you're now suggesting but it didn't exactly turn out that way. I'll find out from the Second Engineer what his plans are and, if he can spare me, I don't mind a spin round the island.'

Whatever the Second had previously in mind, he carefully kept to himself. He obviously sensed the distinct possibility of a chauffered trip and a good day out at minimal expense to himself.

'Well, Third, I don't think there'll be much opportunity to progress the Chief's maintenance programme here. I'll just confirm with him that we can take a break tomorrow,' he advised me.

The Chief didn't raise any objection but when I informed the Second Mate of the good news, his reaction to the Second Engineer inviting himself along was entirely predictable.

'Cheeky sod,' he pronounced. 'You know I'm not switched on to his way of thinking but I suppose I can stomach his company for a few hours ashore.'

'Right, Dave, as soon as we've moored, I'll go to the same garage that I used last time and hire a car for tomorrow. It's only about ten minutes' walk from the berth.'

As it turned out, the Second Engineer turned over a new leaf as far as the Second Mate was concerned, even contributing knowledge accumulated from his previous naval visits to the island many years previously.

'Where next, Dave?' I asked after we'd visited yet another of the first-rate hotels which proliferated around the northern coast.

'Talk about being spoilt for choice. How about driving round to the southern coast, or have you had enough?'

'I don't mind at all. But if I was in your position, I wouldn't know which to choose out of the lot we've seen so far. I can't help but think if we look at any more, you'll be left in even more doubt.'

'Yes, I guess you're right. Let's call it a day and head back to Valletta for a meal. I know just the place for a good nosh.'

After returning to the vessel a couple of hours later, it seemed logical to ask the Second Mate what his choice of hotel was going to be.

'Which is it going to be then, Dave?' I fancied the Luxor Splendour at the North Bay, myself,' I added.

'Yes, once again, I guess you could be right. But when you look at their prices, so it should be, I reckon,' he said.

I somehow had a feeling that our grand tour had not proved as helpful as he'd hoped.

Looking back on that particular excursion, there was no doubt at all that it was a relief from the pressures at that time. Any opportunity to break free from the demanding and regimented life on board, if only for a few hours, counted for a great deal. The country lanes, being almost traffic-free, allowed a freedom of transit that had almost disappeared in the UK apart from in the more remote areas. Whilst the scenery was not always the most spectacular, the coastal roads and views were quite breathtaking, with the hotels providing the jewel in the crown.

It was not long after this excursion that my enthusiasm for life on board this particular vessel started to nosedive in no uncertain terms. Whilst I would normally have been quite reasonably looking forward to berthing at Sicilian ports, this voyage I could barely wait for all of this to be behind us and for us to be homeward bound.

I suppose what was getting to me most was all the uncertainty, particularly with regard to getting relieved for a break or to take study leave on reaching the UK. It was as if one had to take pot luck, with there being no guarantee whatsoever that luck would prevail. I felt my personal life was following a roller-coaster ride but with more downs than ups, unfortunately. There seemed to be an urgent need for me to make more progress with my studies and sit more exams if I intended to get fully certificated within a reasonable period of time. At least then I could start making decisions as to whether to stay at sea or seek a shore vocation, if only to improve my prospects in the long term.

'Studying again, Paul? You're becoming a regular little bookworm,' commented the Second Mate when he appeared at my cabin door the evening after we had berthed in Palermo. 'I'm after a bit of reading matter myself but strictly nothing to do with the job. I thought you would have been tripping the light fantastic tonight, not smothering your head in books.'

'Well, Dave, I've been doing a spot of soul-searching just recently. The way things are going in this game, you just get mucked around by the company when you return to the UK. There's no way of getting any scheduled leave for study, so I've commenced a do-it-yourself drill. Hopefully I will be able to cram enough into my thick head to fool the examiners I'm a fully fledged Electro-technician and Naval Architect, at least to Second Class Part B examination requirements.'

'All I can say is the best of luck, mate. Sounds as if you'll need it,' he added.

Once I had got settled down into a steady pattern, taking a chapter at a time, the course work started to make reasonable sense, certainly better than the first time when I was at college. At least with private study one sets one's own pace, although problem-solving can get extremely frustrating if the answers don't emerge within an acceptable period of time.

The Chief Engineer for one was suitably impressed by my efforts. 'I see you've joined the literary ranks, Third. Would I be right in thinking that you're getting somewhat fed up with the poor relief system at present? I would guess that anybody wanting study leave at the present time has about as much chance as a cow jumping over the moon.'

'Right first time, Chief. I only wish the watch hours were more suitable for studying.'

The Chief's remarks about me joining the literary ranks set me thinking. He seemed to spend endless hours at his typewriter. Whether it be morning, afternoon or evening, whenever one had occasion to visit the Chief's cabin, he seemed to be continually producing reams of paperwork, far more than one would normally expect. In normal circumstances, the majority of his typewritten work would be produced by a chief engineer during the later stages of a voyage, in some instances produced desperately at the last minute, just before berthing in the UK. I was to find out in the not too distant future that the Chief's handiwork had little to do with marine-related matters.

At least the time passed reasonably quickly. As we did not proceed to Messina, our homeward passage to London was well on schedule and we berthed on Christmas morning, much to everyone's relief. We thanked our lucky stars that the lock gate staff were on duty as normal because we were the only vessel due.

15

The comment that greeted the Superintendent's announcement when he boarded the vessel shortly after docking truly summed up our thoughts, reflecting our almost fatalistic resignation of the situation: 'Tell us something new for heaven's sake.' Once again, no reliefs were available but we had the company's blessing to abandon ship over the Christmas period as they had arranged for adequate engine room and watchmen cover, with only one mate and one engineer required to be available for emergency situations.

At first it looked as if I might be lucky enough again to escape to Kent along with the Chief Engineer. That was until I was informed by the Mate of British Rail's decision to give all their staff a day off for the first time, which meant, of course, no trains anywhere. The Chief managed to persuade his wife to drive up to London, against her better inclinations.

'Right,' announced the Fourth Engineer. 'I've bloody well had enough. We're going to have a party on board this ruddy ship tonight that will go down in the annals of history. The biggest orgy this side of Pompeii, if I have anything to do with it.'

His plan of campaign, whilst lacking originality, possibly had a remote chance of success – although quite how he was going to smuggle a bevy of nurses from the local hospital past the dock gate security personnel, nobody could work out.

'Just leave it to me,' he demanded. 'I'll fix the talent. You lot organise the rest, and don't let me down, OK?'

The Fourth certainly wasn't joking. But his determination not to be defeated sounded a few warning bells in the ears of the rest of us.

'Len, you've got to admit you're not the most subtle of guys when it comes to inviting the opposite sex into your parlour,' I ventured. 'It's one thing tempting fate when you're in a face-to-face situation, but you'll surely get the big switch-off if you try it on the phone.'

Those of us who had been in his presence on previous occasions when he was making overtures to females often marvelled at his audacity, but then again, his good looks and charm obviously did the trick as his claimed success rate was well in excess of the rest of us put together.

Whatever Len said was never disclosed. There again, it hardly mattered. The shrieks of laughter as three taxis disgorged their passengers at the foot of our gangway early that evening had us all rushing out on deck to witness his accomplishment. There was no doubt at all that these lasses had just finished their stint for the day at the hospital and couldn't wait to get launched into whatever was on offer on board our fair vessel.

The Chief Steward had, very fortunately, organised the food and drinks with the permission of the Captain, who had been invited to a shore engagement.

The Second Engineer decided to offer his services as barman, which immediately prompted thoughts in my mind about what happened down the Mediterranean on a previous occasion when another engineer of the same rank performed this task, much to my chagrin.

I decided to just let things roll and see what happened. Despite having worked a full shift, our guests were determined to let their hair down, and it soon became obvious that we were becoming spectators to an abundance of dance activity sadly lacking our involvment.

The Fourth suddenly appeared, as if from nowhere, accompanied by one of the more delectable beauties and pronounced in his strong Yorkshire voice above the deafening music, 'Come on, for Pete's sake, it's Christmas night. Let's have some action, you guys.'

'Here, here,' chorused our guests.

It was at this point that the deck department suddenly came to their senses. What followed was a reasonable rendition of a hilarious monologue more usually associated with an infamous lighthouse keeper who had ambitions about the opposite sex way beyond reasonable expectations. This was followed by a few choice verses from 'Nellie Dean', with the gathered throng adding a few extra decibels.

At least the Mates efforts were rewarded with a warm response from our guests and clamours for more of the same. Up to that point in the proceedings, the engineers seemed to be getting off very lightly, but that wouldn't probably last. It was around then I realised that one particular pair of eyes had been focussing in my direction. In fact it was only when I looked her straight in the eyes and she looked away that I was conscious she was probably weighing up what capability I had in the way of entertainment. I decided there was no time like the present to acquaint the lady with my singular lack of expertise, at least of a vocal nature. This was just in case there were demands for me to perform under threat of some dire penalty. I didn't want to have a Christmas to remember for the wrong reasons. I made my way across the lounge in her direction.

'Your glass is looking extremely empty, if you don't mind me saying,' I volunteered. 'What can I tempt you with?'

'I guess you want to get me drunk as a lord,' she replied. 'You sailors are all the same, aren't you?'

'Chance would be a fine thing. What's it to be then, you temptress?' I persevered.

'Just borrow a bottle of gin from the bar and let's take a breath of fresh air on deck.'

And that was where I got my first surprise. No, she wasn't a nurse, just a friend of one. She worked in a large department store in London and had emigrated to the UK from Australia. Her name was Nicolaitta, not Nicola, which her Australian mother would have preferred. But having an

Italian father meant that he didn't want want her to have an Italian male christian name.

'Paul, it's a little too cool for me out here. Let's find ourselves an empty passenger cabin and talk in there.'

'I think you know something I don't, Nicolaitta,' I replied. 'The passenger cabins are usually locked in port, but you never know.'

Obviously, word had reached her one way or another because not just one but all of the passenger cabins were accessible.

We did chat for a while but not for long.

'I think that's enough, Paul. The others will wonder where the heck we are. We'd better get back to the crowd before they send out a search party.'

I reluctantly agreed and we rejoined the others, who didn't even appear to have noticed that we'd been missing for about an hour. They certainly liked their music played excessively loud and neither of us were in the mood for that much volume. She grabbed my hand and we departed once again.

'I've always wanted to invite someone to my cabin to see my etchings,' I ventured. 'The only problem is that I'm not well endowed with artistic accomplishments.'

'You could have fooled me. No, really, I don't know what you're talking about,' she giggled.

I led her down to our accommodation alleyway. Everything was quiet and peaceful; hopefully it would remain that way. Once again the cruel hand of fate was about to intervene, this time in the guise of the Second Engineer. Hardly had we entered my cabin and flung off our outer garments than the door burst open and he entered, drink in hand, to continue his evening's entertainment in our presence.

'Paul, it really is time I was on my way. We talked about ordering a taxi to get back and I'd better see what the other girls are doing.'

I couldn't help but think that until the unfortunate intervention of my collegue, that was about the last thing on her mind.

'Come on then, Nicolaitta, I'll try and get you back to sanity.' But I felt more like jumping into the dock.

16

Christmas 1964 was certainly memorable for all the wrong reasons. Not only had the Second Engineer frustrated my few and sparse moments of happiness with the opposite sex on board the vessel, an action which was to remain a bone of contention between us until my departure, but my girlfriend and family in Kent were more than a little disappointed and surprised at my failure to appear despite arriving in London on Christmas morning.

When I did finally manage to break free and make the journey to Kent, the Christmas spirit was already waning. My brave attempts to rekindle the atmosphere did not prove all that successful. My girlfriend suspected there was more to the matter of my non-appearance than could be attributed to British Rail's failure to provide a train for me to travel on. Of one thing I felt certain: it would soon be time to request the company to relieve me. One way or another, I needed a change of faces and vessel, and to complete my examinations for my Second Class Certificate of Competency.

'Chief, I'm writing to the office for a relief at the end of the next voyage. I reckon I can squeeze in a few weeks at college before the Easter recess to catch up with my studies,' I suggested.

'The way things are going at present with reliefs, Third, I reckon you'll more than probably be disappointed,' the Chief replied.

Our departure being so close to Christmas meant that we had no passengers and not a great deal of cargo either. I was still feeling a little aggrieved about the raw deal we had experienced over the Christmas period and was not filled with enthusiasm about the forthcoming voyage.

Our voyage itinerary was not a great deal different to previous voyages, but in addition to our usual ports of Benghazi, Messina and Malta, we were due to visit Merla Brega, Katakalm and Piraeus, which introduced some additional interest.

Having taken the decision to try to leave the vessel at the end of the voyage, it was time to arrange a further revision programme for my studies. The amount of work to cover for the exam syllabus was nothing short of daunting. Simply having a working knowledge of electrical systems and circuitry and a basic knowledge of ship construction and naval architecture was certainly not sufficient to satisfy the examiners of the Board of Trade, as it was known at that time.

Once launched on my studies, I soon became almost a hermit, with off watch hours flying by with the greatest of ease. I even resisted the temptation of a night ashore in Benghazi

'Paul, you're becoming a social leper. All this studying is a ruddy waste of time, if you ask me. By the time you're sat in the exam room, you'll have forgotten the lot.' The Fourth Engineer was no bookworm. All his inspiration emanated from a beer bottle, and as far as he was concerned, all I was doing was wasting valuable drinking time.

'Len, I just happen to believe about the only way I'll progress up the ranks is to do it myself, so to speak. Getting time off for college study is bloody hopeless at present. I'm sorry if it gets up your nose but I'll promise you this: if we can get a night ashore in Piraeus, I'll leave the books behind. How about that? And, in the meantime, help yourself to my top end spanner and a bottle to go with it.'

'That sounds like a ruddy poor compromise to me, but who's going to argue when I'm about to swipe one of your beers.'

I broke off my studies and we sat and chatted about our respective futures. Len had no intention of achieving anything more than a regular payment into his bank account in return for his undoubtedly useful contribution to keeping the ship on the move. Provided that he was able to partake, at regular intervals, of the delights of the opposite sex, it seemed his life was complete.

My own horizon extended a little further down the road, and whilst I shared his enthusiasm for the opposite sex, I just felt the need to prove at least to myself that I could complete a course of study and achieve a goal. This wasn't so easy to do when one's life was dictated by the need to be chasing after every bit of skirt that loomed into view.

Len summed up our considered opinions as the evening wore on.

'You'll probably end up making a small pile but be as miserable as sin, whereas I, my son, will die broke but with a smile on my face.'

'Yes, I wouldn't doubt that, Len, but I bet the only way I'll make a pile is to win the pools. Anyway, I'm turning in now, my buddy, if you don't mind, otherwise you won't get relieved at midnight.'

After a short stopover at Merla Brega on the North African coast, we proceeded towards Piraeus.

As usual, after completing my afternoon watch and before getting a shower, I handed in the log books to the Chief Engineer. At least that was my intention, but there was no sign of him. I checked his bathroom and bedroom but he wasn't around. Judging by his desk and particularly his typewriter, he had been interrupted in the middle of quite a lengthy diatribe. My curiosity was aroused. Glancing at the material in the typewriter, I gasped. Had my eyes deceived me. No. Cor blimey, this was too hot to handle. I wouldn't have even guessed that the Chief had such a vivid imagination or the descriptive talent to be able to compile such material. Probably it was autobiographical, and the thought made me convulse into hysterical laughter, just as I heard his familiar footsteps resounding down the alleyway. Ye Gods, talk about being caught in the act.

'Are, there you are, Chief. The Fourth can't half tell them. Dear, or dear, if I don't get to the bathroom quickly, it'll be too late.'

With that, I threw the log books at the Chief and departed the scene faster than the speed of sound.

I could only imagine that the Chief had a very profitable outlet for his handiwork, probably even earned him more than his renumeration as a Chief Engineer.

If the Chief suspected I'd been eavesdropping on his undoubted talent as an author, he didn't reveal this to me. I decided to keep my revelation to myself, otherwise the Chief would put two and two together and my secret would be out.

'Where the hell is the Chief Steward obtaining his supplies, I wonder? I'm sure he's trying to finish us off.' The Second Mate was airing his views, once again, in the saloon.

'Look, Dave, short of eating all one's meals ashore, which does present obvious problems, there's precious little we can do about the situation. I think the Cook isn't that happy about his raw materials either but I bet he's still sharing in the profits from the sale of our original stores.'

Our arrival in Piraeus was more than welcome, if only to break the monotony of our seagoing routine. Then the Second Engineer warned us that he would be expecting us to perform miracles down below as there would probably be little further opportunity to carry out routine maintenance duties.

'Paul, I've had a word with the Second. He's agreed to us having a night ashore tomorrow night, if we're still here. OK?'

'Knowing our luck, Len, we'll be on our way to our next port.'

We toiled long and hard that day and hoped for the best. But our luck held, mainly due to the lack of enthusiasm of the stevedores, who still appeared to be on their Christmas holidays.

'Where are we bound then, Paul?' enquiried the Fourth Engineer as we headed down the gangway.

'Depends on what you're after,' I replied. 'We can stay in the local bars in Piraeus or go uptown. There's supposed to be plenty of nightlife, Greek-style, in the old quarter not far from the Acropolis. If my memory serves me right, they call it the Plaka or something like that.'

'As long as there's food, beer and a bird or two, in that order, that's fine by me.'

After one for the road locally, we boarded our train for the short journey to the metropolis. What a relief it was to be ashore, I just hoped that our expectations would be fulfilled, at least foodwise.

17

Although I could not claim to understand Len's reasoning at times, of one thing I was certain, he was a great believer in acting on impulse. So be it as we wandered through the Plaka.

We were almost swamped in a seething mass of humanity that had congregated in the narrow streets. The charming surroundings with old mansions and houses side by side vying with picturesque taverns on almost every street corner and the sweet smell of the jasmin bushes and basil pots in the courtyards were no compensation. Len had had enough.

'Right, Paul, in here for God's sake. Looks OK to me.'

There was no doubt at all that his choice of eating venue had been more determined by the pressure surrounding us than any other factor.

'Judging by the looks on the faces of those around us, Len, we've either interrupted a meeting of their secret society or we've descended from another planet.'

'Sod them, all I want is a ruddy beer right now, and if that fancy-dressed little git over there doesn't get his backside round here, I shall . . .'

'Yes, what will you do?' I enquired.

Fortunately for us, the waiter decided it was time to act his part.

'Good evening, gentlemen. May I welcome you to our tavern. Our food is very good, our refreshments are even better and our entertainment the best in Athens. You have chosen well.'

With that, he departed from the scene gesticulating at his staff like a frenetic madman.

'Looks as if we'll have to mortgage the vessel to pay off our bill tonight, Len. Talk about dropping ourselves in the proverbial. Ah well, in for a drachma, in for a million or two.'

A look of considerable concern was spreading over Len's face and my attempt to lighten the situation was not proving effective.

'How much cash have you?' he enquired.

'Around thirty pounds, if you must know. Also about ten pounds' worth of drachmas.'

'Well, we should be all right then.' He seemed extremely relieved.

'How about you? Let's hear the worst,' I asked.

But before he could answer, an equally flamboyantly dressed waiter presented himself, complete with menu and a wine list.

'Can I have a bloody beer pronto, matey,' demanded Len in his broad West Yorkshire accent, much to the bewilderment of the waiter.

Speedy intervention on my part was obviously urgently required.

'My friend is enquiring about the availability of a beer,' I tried. This sounded just about as clear as Len's diatribe, but fortunately the drachma dropped.

'Sorry, my dear sir, we have no beer but very good wine and other special drinks. You Americans will love our good drinks,' he insisted.

Len and I hadn't a clue what to order. Len was almost past caring. To be mistaken for an American was almost the last straw, as his grimace clearly demonstrated.

'Please bring us a bottle of your good quality drink and then we will order our food,' I decided.

'I hope you bloody well know what you're doing, Paul. They could end up poisoning us and we wouldn't know.'

'Well, if they do, my friend, it won't really matter anyway.

At least we shall be saved the monotony of the return voyage to the UK, present company excepted,' I replied.

'Right, be it on your head. What's on the ruddy menu? Anything we can recognise?'

'Hell, Len, it's all Greek to me. Nothing in English. Blimey, haven't we landed ourselves in it.'

'Go on, remind me. It was my idea, wasn't it ...' but before he could say any more, a voice from an adjacent table interrupted our dialogue.

'Couldn't help but hear your plight. You are obviously English and a little far from home. Let me introduce myself.'

We both swung around in our chairs to confront the source of the very English voice that sounded like music in our ears.

'How do you do. I am Christopher, head of English studies at the Naval Museum College. This fair lady along-side me is Diana, my wife. Who do I have the pleasure of talking to?'

'Well, I'm Paul and my friend here is Leonard. We're officers from the good vessel *Leo* currently berthed in the harbour at Piraeus. At least, it was a couple of hours or so ago when we came ashore.'

We shook hands, admitted to our almost total ignorance of Greek culinary delights and liquid refreshment to suit, and within minutes had been more than adequately informed about the best grub in town which we would have the good fortune to partake of.

It was apparent that Christopher and his good lady were regular customers of what was undoubtedly an excellent establishment, and after a brief discussion he had a word in the ear of the head waiter, who reappeared with the wine waiter. Almost instantaneously a large bottle of clear liquid in an amazingly decorated bottle appeared on our table, together with a decanter of iced water. We thanked our benefactor for his kind assistance and just hoped that we had chosen well.

'What the hell do they provide iced water for, Paul? We didn't ask for it, did we?'

'No, but just try a drop of the other liquid then I guess you may have an answer to your own question.'

His face was a picture growing more ruddy by the second as he gasped after quaffing a sizeable gulp of the admittedly quiet-looking drink. He grabbed the decanter and poured an even greater quantity of the iced water down his gullet, much to the amusement of all around.

'Len, for heaven's sake, you're going to be the cabaret if you repeat that performance.'

He was still recovering his equilibrium and hadn't spoken another word by the time our food arrived.

'Bloody hell, Paul ... that's fire water. Nearly burnt a hole in my larynx. Let's hope the food isn't full of spice, otherwise my guts will end up as me garters.'

But the food was magnificent. Our benefactor had advised us well. We also soon learnt the technique with the liquid refreshments, but even then there was no doubt at all about the potency of the non-iced liquid.

'That's the food taken care of, Paul. Not so sure about the drinks, but guess we'll survive. What about the women? Bit of a sod really having friend Christopher and his spouse breathing down our necks, don't you agree? It's like having big brother watching over you.'

'Yes, I guess so, but we can hardly expect them to bugger off just for our convenience. There isn't that amount of talent around, anyway. In fact, the most likely lasses, I reckon, are those three sat together at the table just to the right of the cabaret floor.'

'That's no bloody good. There's only the two of us. Oh, sod it, let's enjoy the entertainment and we'll go from there, eh.'

There was no doubt in Len's mind about what was to follow. Probably he would have reacted differently if he had been forewarned. On the other hand, Len enjoyed living life to the full whenever possible.

In the beginning, the musicians were almost withdrawn, with little to indicate what was to follow. But before too long, with audience participation increasing by the minute, the whole atmosphere rapidly changed. As if by magic, costumed dancers appeared from nowhere. The tempo and volume of the music literally took off and before we had time to adjust, a crescendo of sound, together with matching action and lighting, almost drowned us.

'By gum, me old matey,' bawled Len at the limit of his vocal chords, 'there's plenty of life in this old town, judging from this bunch.'

Len's liquid intake had been steadily increasing at the same pace as the tempo of the entertainment, so it should have come as no surprise that he would wish to join the cabaret. There was just no way that the refrains of 'Ilkley Moor baht 'at' would be a hit in a Greek tavern, but at least he had tried.

18

Paradoxically, it was only when we were drinking cups of strong black coffee in the messroom next day that it began to dawn on the Fourth Engineer that his vocal talents were not everybodys cup of tea – and certainly not appreciated by the good folks present in the tavern the previous night. In fact, he had still been rendering a version of his favourite anthem as a taxi arrived to transport us back to our good vessel, with our new friends undoubtedly more than relieved to see the back of us.

'For Pete's sake, Paul, you should have stopped me making a fool of myself. Hells' bells, I shan't want to bump into the professor and his bird again. Anyway, it's all history now. I still think there was nowt wrong with me refrain,' pleaded Len.

'For crying out loud, of course there's nothing wrong with the basic refrain, provided you stick to the original version, but believe you me, you bloody well murdered it and you didn't have to be Greek to weigh that up,' I responded. 'As for stopping you, you must be joking. When you're steaming along at full boiler pressure, not even a brick wall would stop you.'

I glanced across at him. A look of deep concern had spread over his face.

'Eh dear, me old buddy, I'm going to have to change my bloody ways. That's what my girlfriend back home keeps saying. Guess she must be right.'

'Len, the day you change your ways will be the day I land on the moon,' I responded.

'Thanks a million, I appreciate your confidence, mate.'

The news that we were next proceeding to Malta brought back memories of our previous foray ashore in a hired car, but any thoughts of being able to repeat our little adventure were soon dashed by the Chief Engineer insisting that we try to catch up on our maintenance schedule.

As it turned out, we were not able to achieve a great deal down below because of the requirement to keep the main engines ready for shifting ship, which, once again, did not please the Chief.

'You know, Third, the company's going to have to think about investing in some new cargo ships. This type of vessel is fine if you have the opportunity to look after the machinery, but with the short stopovers we're having in ports these days, there just isn't sufficient time to do the job properly.'

'I guess you're referring to the bridge-controlled vessels with all the latest remote monitoring gear, Chief. They'll probably try and do away with engineers on board next,' I added sarcastically.

'That will be the day, Third. Over my dead body,' he replied.

Neither of us was aware at that time of the company's well-advanced plans for not only a whole new class of sophisticated cargo vessels to ply mainly the Mediterranean ports, but also for a large new passenger ferry vessel to serve the Scandinavian ports.

From Malta our last port of call was Messina. I resisted the temptation to venture ashore despite knowing this could well be the last opportunity for some time to partake of the unique atmosphere of this Sicilian port.

'Come on, Paul. We're only popping down to that bistro outside the harbour.' The Second Mate, together with the Fourth Engineer, couldn't believe my reluctance to step ashore.

'You two aren't proposing to be sitting exams in the near future. Go and enjoy yourselves and have one on me,' I suggested.

I actually managed to organise my future study schedule and after a nightcap, duly turned in with the intention of enjoying a precious night's sleep.

As they say, the best laid plans of mice and men . . .

At first I thought I was dreaming. Then a feeling of déjà vu quickly reminded me that I was now, regrettably, wide awake. The refrain blasting its way down the quay towards the vessel was definitely of Yorkshire origin, emanating from somewhere in the region of Ilkley. It sounded no better than it did in that Athenian eating house except that this time it was accompanied by a cacophony of whistles, shouts, trumpets and horns of mixed origin. Thank God, we had no passengers on board. The deafening noise was enough to waken the metropolis.

There was almost an inevitability that I would be favoured with a visit from our intrepid troubadours, therefore I wasted no time in vacating my bunk.

'Welcome back on board the good ship *Leo*,' I announced as I pulled my door open just nicely in time to see them fall in a heap on my doormat.

'Bloody hell,' announced the Fourth from the bottom of the pile. 'I've managed to stay on my ruddy feet all night. Where the hell did the floor go?'

'Never mind about that. Where did your instrumental support come from and where have they gone?' I enquired.

The Second Mate surfaced and took up the story.

'That lot were in the pub. They liked Len's vocal offering and invited themselves back on board. Unfortunately for them, harbour security decided differently. Such is life,' he shrugged.

'Well, as you're here and I'm not in there,' pointing to my bunk, 'what's your tipple?'

'Thought you were never going to ask,' chimed in the Fourth.

I hadn't a great deal to offer drinkwise, so they helped

90

themselves to a pale ale and then decided they would try and put the world right, or at least the bit of it that concerned them.

'What do you reckon to all these great plans the company has announced for new vessels, Paul? We shall soon be able to dispense with engineers, if you believe all the spiel that's being bandied about,' the Second Mate added, somewhat mercilessly.

'One thing you can be sure about, Dave, they will definitely cut back on seagoing staff, but as for doing away with engineers, I don't reckon that will mean there'll be much saving made. Look what we have to fix at present. Cost them a fortune if they had to bring in repairers each time a problem cropped up. You guys are not in a hurry to get your hands mucky, let's face it.'

'I'll second that,' chimed in Len. 'You practically need us to open your bloody beer cans now, you do. As for fixing things in the engine room, eh by gum, laddy, that would be a sight for sore eyes.'

Dave was taking our chiding with infinite patience but even he had heard enough.

'If jumbo planes can fly round the world without an engineer on board, it won't be long before ships follow suit, I reckon,' proposed the Second Mate.

'One problem with that argument,' Len dived in, 'it's bloody hard to fix an engine in mid-air, so they design 'em to fly on the rest. If your ship's engine breaks down, you're going nowhere, and tugs don't come cheap.'

'Come off it, Len. Ships are being built these days with more than one engine, so surely that's no problem,' Dave challenged.

I was quite enjoying my colleagues' argument but I couldn't help but think they were both missing the main point.

'Come on, you two. It's a case of horses for courses, surely. Let's face it, I've been up on the bridge in bad weather, thick fog and heavy traffic conditions when I've thanked God I haven't had to be responsible for the safety of the ship. Equally, Dave, wild horses wouldn't have dragged you into the back end of boilers still under steam pressure, to try and expand leaking boiler tubes, I reckon.'

'True enough, but the shipowner is only interested in how cheaply he can run his ships, and if that means sacrificing any of us, that for sure is what will happen.'

'I'm prepared to settle for that profound observation, my dear chap, if only so I can retire to my bunk, if you don't mind,' I pleaded.

Fortunately, the message got through and my two colleagues departed forthwith.

19

'Are we actually on a homeward passage now, Dave?' I enquired of the Second Mate next day as we headed towards the North African coast westward bound. 'Whatever happened to Merla Brega and Katakalm, wherever they're supposed to be?'

'Yes, we sure are. London next stop, hopefully. No cargo for us at the other ports you mentioned. Once again, our itinerary was changed, no doubt to suit some agent who happens to be the flavour of the month with the company, but that upsets shippers at the other ports and they get their cargo transferred to other vessels.'

I settled into a routine of watchkeeping, studying and just enough social contact with my fellow officers to convince them that I hadn't turned into an academic zombie.

Even the weather managed to co-operate, with the usual splendid conditions along the Mediterranean then out to Cape St Vincent, but as we headed towards the Bay of Biscay dark, grey, dismal skies descended in our direction, with the wind and sea strength increasing in intensity.

'Are we far from Ushant, Dave?' I asked, trying to work out our ETA for London, with the thought in mind of whether or not my relief would meet the vessel.

'If this weather doesn't moderate, we've another day's steaming before we pass Ushant, then it's about a day and a half to London, which means an arrival early a.m. tide this coming Sunday.'

'Bugger me, that will mean I shan't see my relief until Monday. Still, the Chief might agree to my popping down to my sister's in Kent and I might even be lucky enough to see my girlfriend before I head home.'

The weather improved a little but not sufficiently to enable us to make up for lost time and, sure enough, just as the Second Mate had predicted, we berthed in the Millwall Dock on the early Sunday morning tide with not a soul to be seen on the quay.

Not for the first time, on appearing at my sister's front door several hours later, I was greeted with, 'Where the heck have you sprung from, Paul? We thought you were still down the Mediterranean. Anyway, it's great to see you. Come on in and I'll fix you some breakfast.'

'Sorry I didn't ring you to let you know we'd arrived but I didn't think you would appreciate a telephone call at four thirty this morning when we docked, and by the time the Chief had made up his mind to let me come, I just had enough time to get to Victoria Station to catch the next train.'

As usual, our conversation revolved around the family and all the latest dramas that seemed to descend on them with unfailing frequency.

'Paul, do you keep in contact with Christine? She told me recently that she hasn't had a letter from you since Christmas and wondered if all was well with you,' my sister enquired.

'To be honest, Jennifer, after the Christmas cock-up with our reliefs and the rather luke-warm reception I got afterwards, I guessed Christine was not exactly over the moon with me. I nearly wrote to her but changed my mind, which obviously hasn't helped matters at all.'

'I'll leave it to you, but I do think she would like you to contact her, and as you're here and she is only five minutes away, surely it wouldn't do any harm to give her a ring.'

'When I remind her that I'm returning home on Monday and going back to college to continue my studies, I can't imagine that will make me her favourite friend,' I replied.

I could see that for the sake of friendly family relationships I would have to carry out my dear sister's wishes so, following a very welcome breakfast, I dialled my girlfriend's number and waited with some trepidation for a response.

'Hello there, it's the Lone Ranger,' I blurted out before I realised the voice on the other end was not Christine's.

'It's not the stables at Laramie and we ain't seen Tonto,' replied the male voice, which I didn't immediately recognise.

'Sorry, I know your voice but I just can't place you. I'm Paul. Is Christine around, please?'

'She's around but in the bathroom, I think. Are you at your sister's house, Paul?' he asked.

'Yes, that's right. It's Christine's uncle, isn't it?'

'It certainly is. I'll get her to ring you when she's out of the bath,' he replied.

It seemed an eternity before my sister's telephone rang.

'Hi, Paul here. How is my favourite girlfriend?' was the best response I could think of.

'You are a cheeky so-and-so, Paul, if you don't mind my saying. I'm OK, I suppose, but why haven't you been in touch with me since Christmas? I've missed hearing from you.'

'All I can do is apologise to you, Christine. I guessed you weren't too impressed with my poor response over Christmas but that wasn't my fault. I'm afraid problems like that crop up with our way of life. Anyway, I'd love to see you if you're free.'

'How long are you around for?' she asked.

'Only today. I've got to be back on board the vessel first thing in the morning to meet my relief then I'm away back home to continue my studies,' I replied.

'Nothing changes, does it, Paul? Anyway, if you like to drop round early afternoon, I'll probably have had sufficient time to reschedule my day.'

'Great, I'll look forward to that. See you then, Christine.'

My brother-in-law had partly overheard my telephone

conversation and very kindly offered me the use of his car for the afternoon.

'It had better arrive back here in the same condition that it leaves or begorrah, I'll have your legs for lunch,' he chided.

Fortunately, I had previously owned the same model of car, so familiarity was no problem – and I knew the roads like the back of my hand.

We had a great afternoon visiting a couple of well-loved watering holes deep in the heart of the Kent countryside until closing time, then made our way to our favourite eating house not a million miles from Canterbury.

'I must ring my sister and let her know I shan't be back for a meal,' I announced, then disappeared to the lobby to make the call.

The only surprise for me that afternoon was how quiet Christine was, certainly not her usual bubbly self, and I remarked on this to my sister when she asked me how things were going during my call.

'All I can say is that you must be losing your touch, or words to that effect,' my sister joked.

On rejoining Christine at our table, I sensed that a few soul-searching questions were shortly going to be heading in my direction.

For once I was right, but it was only when we were about to leave and head back to her home that Christine grabbed my hand and, out of the blue, asked me if I loved her. I promised her I would answer that question as soon as I knew the answer, which could be on the way home. Almost before the words were out of my mouth, I regretted saying them but there was no going back now.

'Pull over, Paul, in the woods. Surely we've time to talk before heading back.'

'Yes, sure thing, although I only have the car until early evening. Mind you, we're only twenty minutes from base.'

I decided that I was in a no-win situation and just hoped that fortune would favour the brave.

'How could any red-blooded man resist such a dazzlingly

beautiful, delectfully delightful young lady as you, especially when she asks you if you love her. To be honest, my love, you deserve better than me and my ruddy job . . .'

I didn't get a chance to continue the dialogue.

I was still feeling in seventh heaven as I pulled the car onto my sister's drive after promising my girlfriend that I would keep in close contact with her despite the distance that was to separate us for the foreseeable future.

'Jennifer, I think you could be seeing a lot more of me if I'm able to get a southern-based vessel after I've finished my next study period,' I told her.

It didn't take her very long to put two and two together.

Then my brother-in-law appeared, looking extremely serious and holding an unmistakeable article of women's clothing in his hand.

'Are you trying to get me a divorce, Paul? Anyway, thanks for returning my car intact, at least externally. I'll say no more to spare your blushes.'

It was with mixed feelings that I departed next day, homeward bound on the train from London after bidding farewell to my shipmates for the last time.

20

It was April 1965. I had just two months to achieve an exam pass standard, which I reckoned was cutting things a trifle close but hopefully my previous work at sea would help me to speed through the college studies.

I had barely commenced at college when it soon became apparent that I was not going to be left alone by my friends to concentrate on the job in hand. It was the frequency of the phone calls that led me to believe that probably it would have been better if I had chosen to study at a college away from home. After all, there was a good choice of colleges spread right round the country which catered especially for Merchant Navy Officers studying for their engineering Certificates of Competency.

My dear mother was, once again, stepping in on my behalf to intercept as many calls as possible but even she was vulnerable to a surprise, out-of-the-blue call.

She came into my study one evening. 'Guess who that was on the phone, Paul?' she exclaimed, with a look of bewilderment on her face.

I looked suitably bemused, half expecting her to name some long lost friend.

'That was Diane. She asked me to give you a message. She's getting engaged next month and will be living in London again and just wanted to wish you well with your exams.'

I couldn't help but feel that time and events were passing me by with a bewildering speed. Was I destined to be a bookworm, for ever aloof to life around me, whilst I attempted to achieve the unattainable?

'Cheer up, Paul. You look like a dog that's lost its tail. There are plenty of very nice girls around who would give their left arm to get their hands on you, but only if you remain in contact with them.'

'It's funny you should say that, Mum. I must do that very thing tonight. You remember Christine in Kent, well I saw her briefly before I came home and promised her I would keep in touch.'

'There you are then,' my mother replied. 'But you're not going to be able to see her again for a while, now are you?'

'I guess not. Anyway, we'll just have to wait and see. I might be sailing on a vessel from southern ports after I've finished my exams, then things will be easier in that sense.'

I couldn't help but reflect on the uncertainties of our way of life. It was like taking a ride on a roller coaster, one was never quite sure in which direction life was taking you, who you would meet on the way, the high spots and the disasters and whether or not you would survive to see another day.

Having said that, my main concern was to avoid a disaster in the exam room next time round so I decided to burn a few midnight candles to lessen the risk of that happening.

Time marched steadfastly on, with me at times wondering why the intricacies of naval architecture and electro-technology were proving a trifle more difficult than they should have been. There again, what was becoming increasingly obvious to all of us trying to cram our memories full of all the necessary technical information were the advances that were increasingly being made in the field of electronic systems and equipment, all of which required a working knowledge if one wasn't going to be caught with one's trousers down, technically speaking, at some critical time in the future. Naturally enough, the examiners were keen to make sure that those candidates presenting themselves for examination were fully au fait with all these developments, and our lecturers left us under no doubt whatsoever that unless we demonstrated the gifts of Faraday, we had little chance of succeeding where others had failed. Fortunately, the demands of our naval architecture course were not so daunting, although at times trying to work out what would happen to a vessel when water entered the wrong places was about as difficult as predicting the effects of a failure of some new high-tech piece of engine-monitoring equipment installed supposedly, to take pressure off the watch engineer.

Time would soon tell if our efforts were to be rewarded. I felt reasonably confident this time round but was not over-optimistic about my chances of passing, which would set me on the first rung of success.

'How do you reckon you did then, Paul?' asked one of my former shipmates who was attending college on another course.

It had seemed a long day in the examination room but I had decided to pop back to college to collect a few belongings.

'Not too bad, Simon. I'd expected the worst, particularly with the electro-tech paper, but there were no surprises, thank goodness. So who knows, I might have made it.'

The moment of truth was not too long delayed. Even so, a feeling of trepidation had managed to percolate my inner thoughts. I knew from previous experience that the look on the examination clerk's face would give me a fair indication of how I had done.

A beaming smile lit up his face as he handed me the dreaded piece of paper and my spirits rose.

'Well done, James,' he announced. 'Full steam ahead for your Chief's now, I expect.'

'Yes, I guess so. Anyway, thanks for your congratulations,' I replied. His memory for faces, names and examination results never failed to impress those who had passed through his hands, even those, like me, who had failed on more than one occasion.

I decided to take the clerk's words of wisdom as good

advice and, taking the bull by the horns, asked the company if I could return to college in September to study for part A of the First Class Certificate. I had been exempt from sitting part A of the Second Class Certificate because of previous qualifications, which meant that I had a lot of revising to do to get my theoretical brain cells re-activated. Whether or not it was my sheer downright cheek or a company decision to encourage me, I had no way of knowing, but instead of promoting me straight away, I was offered the chance to relieve the Third Engineer on the *Hydra* so that he could take six weeks leave before I returned to college to continue my studies.

Whilst Christine was pleased about my exam success, she was not over the moon with the arrangements before I returned to college.

'Paul, I remember exactly your words the last time we discussed what you would be doing next.'

'I know, my love, but if I don't take the opportunity to get my qualifications as quickly as possible, I could be left stranded, quite literally. I know I shan't be sailing out of London on the *Hydra* and will probably not be able to return south for a while, but I promise you that I will see you before I return to college in September.'

'Can I rely on what you've just told me, or will you be giving me another excuse next time your circumstances change?' she enquired.

'Yes, you can, and we'll keep in touch on the phone and with letters,' I replied.

I could not help but think that it was not always a question of being caught between the devil and the deep blue sea. Girlfriends could be just as demanding but, of course, for all the right reasons.

It was a great feeling to join my new vessel sailing on the same voyage to Sweden as the *Lara* on which I had served as Fourth Engineer.

Probably even better news was the discovery that my

fellow officers, including the Captain and the Stewardess, held none of the antiquated beliefs that had made my life very difficult indeed on the *Lara*. Indeed, one was actively encouraged to join in the social life on board, provided that did not lead to mayhem and complaints from the passengers.

I could not wait to rediscover the delights of Gothenburg, particularly as the weather was still mild enough to be able to walk around without the risk of suffering the same fate as a particular monkey.

The Chief Engineer was also on board in a relief capacity and more used to the much harder toil that was frequently the engineer's fate on the longer-voyage vessels. He was certainly determined to make the most of his welcome break, with plenty of participation in the social activities in the bar.

'That's it then, Third,' shouted the Second Engineer, as the engine room telegraph swung to Finished with Engines.

We had arrived and berthed in Gothenburg, it seemed almost before we had departed from the UK.

21

I decided that one of the first things I should do once I was able to get ashore would be to buy my girlfriend from Kent a present. Quite what form it would take I hadn't a clue. The Chief Engineer wasn't a great deal of help either.

'Depends of why you are buying her it, Third. But you can't go wrong with perfume in one form or another.'

'Thanks, Chief. She'll probably suggest that I bought it for her because she needs freshening up,' I replied.

'Well, then, Third, how about a sexy negligee? Sounds like she would really have a cracking answer for the reason why you bought her it,' he joked.

'You've put an idea into my head, thanks, Chief. Incidentally, it won't be a negligee,' I told him.

I was soon reminded that breakdowns, whether in the engine room or elsewhere, sometimes required an immediate response. This time it was a true emergency. The bar frig was playing up. From the Chief Steward's point of view, that situation was just as disastrous as the Captain not being able to steer the vessel. At least the working environment was more than friendly with a satisfactory result earning a very welcome liquid refresher and grateful thanks from the catering department. It was just as well I wasn't planning on going ashore that morning even if I'd been given the opportunity.

The problem wasn't going to be resolved in five minutes. I had diagnosed a major component failure, which was extremely unusual, and unique in my experience, with the type of equipment fitted. Fortunately, in the spares locker a new compressor motor was lying in pristine condition, but due to poor access the changeover would take the remainder of the morning.

'Are you winning, Third?' enquired the Chief, as he appeared on the other side of the bar for his pre-lunch appetiser.

'Hopefully, Chief, unless something else crops up during testing,' I replied.

'If all is OK, you can get yourself ashore after lunch. If I remember correctly, you've got a particular piece of shopping to do,' he added.

Fortunately, the equipment worked to the satisfaction and relief of the Chief Steward.

'There'll be a case on its way down to your cabin shortly, Third,' he promised.

'That's very welcome, Chief. It's great to be appreciated,' I replied.

Working for the Catering Department did have its rewards, at least on this good vessel.

I was really looking forward to stepping ashore in Gothenburg, particularly in August. It was only a few minutes' walk into the city centre from the vessel's berth and, once there, the choice of department stores was bewildering.

I knew there would be equally as bewildering a choice of gifts to buy her but I felt certain that a Swedish charm bracelet would probably be more than welcome, judging from the popularity of these bracelets at that time.

'Paul, are you venturing into town?' enquired the Second Engineer.

'Anytime now. Why, are you thinking of coming along, Peter?' I asked.

'Not particularly. I just wondered if you would get me one of those saucy photo mags if you are passing a bookshop,' he asked.

My mind flashed back to some of the publications I had seen when I last sailed to this port.

'Depends on what you call saucy. I certainly won't be buying any of the type that leave absolutely nothing to the imagination,' I responded.

'Looks as if I'm going to have to do my own shopping then. If you hang on for five minutes, I'll join you.'

The fact that photo magazines were on open display depicting performing arts requiring the participants to have been trained by Houdini did not appeal to me in the slightest. Later, as we both headed into town, the Second Engineer reminded me that the Scandinavians were not backward in creating visual displays to celebrate the human anatomy.

'After all, Paul, there's a park in Oslo that has an obelisk about sixty feet high made up of entwining human bodies in the form of a phallic symbol. I haven't seen it myself but I'm told it's very erotic,' he explained.

'Really? I didn't realise the Scandinavians were that artistic. Maybe I'll have a look-see if I ever get to Oslo,' I replied.

It could be said that we were both spoilt for choice with our respective requirements. I just hoped my chosen gift would placate my girlfriend's disappointment with my current sailing arrangements. What she would have made of the Second Engineer's bit of shopping, goodness knows. Anyway, at least he was quite happy with it.

22

I had decided to limit my trips ashore in Gothenburg because the cost of most things, including food, drink, presents, entertainment and almost anything else one could think of, was a lot more than in the UK. I intented to try to save up for a good holiday back home before starting college again, however my lack of self-indulgence was badly misjudged by my fellow officers. Even the Mate, whom I did not know all that well, remarked one day on this apparent change of heart on my part.

'I'm told you're a bit of a lad around town with the girls, Third. Can't say I've seen much evidence to support this while you've been aboard,' he ventured one evening as we shared the Second Mate's hospitality.

'I don't know about that, Chief. It costs a small fortune ashore and I'm trying to impress a girlfriend back home. So, having just spent too much on a gift for her, I'm not spending any more in this fair city this trip. Mind you, I'd like to go back to the Liseberg Amusement Park and pay a visit to the Ullevi Stadium, but that will have to wait until another trip,' I added.

The relaxed routine and predictable work schedule on this vessel was, once again, a reminder of the vast difference in life for engineers on different vessels and different voyages, when compared with the routines of the other crew members. The current routine allowed sufficient time for work, rest and play in very welcome amounts, with everything very spick and span and shipshape.

Whether or not to reveal that I had a surprise for my

106

girlfriend when we next met left me in a state of indecision. In the end, I decided to mention in my next letter to her that I'd done a bit of shopping in a big store and leave it at that.

Our return voyage to the UK was completely uneventful, as usual, with journey's end arriving almost before it had begun. One thing was certain in my mind. Given the right shipmates, this was certainly the life for me. It was a crying shame that it was to be for so short a period of time.

I wondered if I would be pressurised into revealing the nature of my purchase as I dialled my girlfriend's telephone number in Kent that evening. As it happened it didn't matter at all. Her mother answered the phone and rather brusquely advised me that her daughter was out for the evening with her boyfriend. She would pass on my message and good wishes.

I had just replaced the handset when my mother made her presence felt. 'Girlfriend trouble again, Paul?' she queried in her uniquely intuitive way.

'No, not really, but Christine's mum is a bit of a pain in the proverbial, I'm afraid. She isn't all that keen on my vocation. She obviously thinks that a seafarer isn't the right person for her darling daughter. Never mind, we shall see,' I added.

'Paul, for goodness sake, I should just let things quieten down for the time being. After all, you won't be in a position to see her again for a while, will you?' she suggested.

'Guess you're right, Mum, as usual. There again, it's not like you to advise me to do that, now is it?' I replied.

'That's very true, but you hardly know the girl, let's face it.'

I did not enlighten my mother any further in this respect. I could well imagine her imagination running riot with visions of wedding bells ringing prematurely.

Despite trying to contact Christine at her place of work,

she was never available. Could she be having second thoughts, I wondered? If so, then my gift would have been a waste of time, no matter what. I decided to speak to my sister in Kent and try to find out what was really going on.

'Paul. I am afraid to say that you're not exactly the flavour of the month when it comes down to personal relationships with you-know-who and her mum,' my sister advised as tactfully as she could. 'Her mother thinks that your way of life is too disruptive for normal family life to exist,' she added.

'Thanks, Jennifer, for the situation report. By the way, does this boyfriend her mum mentioned, see her regularly?'

'To be perfectly honest, Paul, she knows quite a few young chaps in the Canterbury area but no one seriously as far as I'm aware,' she replied.

'Well, as they say, time will tell, I suppose. Anyway, I'm looking forward to coming down to see you all again in a few weeks' time, as soon as I have completed my relief spell on my current vessel.'

I pondered on what I had just learnt. If she wouldn't even talk to me on the telephone then there was precious little that I could do to change her mind.

At least my new car was proving to be a darn sight more amenable, also reliable. I couldn't wait to be heading south once again, with a mission to accomplish. I hoped to persuade my girlfriend that there was plenty going for us in all respects, all that was needed was a bit of patience for the time being. A chance to establish my credentials, so to speak.

Whether or not my pleas would fall on deaf ears, I couldn't even begin to work out.

23

'Our passengers for this voyage are a real mixed bunch, Paul. They're in a party and apparently like their liquid refreshments, so let's hope the bar frig doesn't let us down any more,' advised the Stewardess, just before we were due to sail.

'As far as I know, Carol, all's well in that department but I will check it again after we've sailed. I'm just about to start the pre-departure checks with the deck department, so I can't deal with it right now,' I replied.

Usually about an hour before we sailed, testing of the main engines, steering systems, alarm and monitoring systems, also the bridge and engine room communication systems, including the engine telegraph was carried out in conjunction with the deck department and the respective timepieces synchronised.

Judging by the crescendo of laughter that ricocheted around the upper decks, it sounded as if our passengers were really getting into the swing of things.

It was a Friday evening departure, which meant that with good weather on passage we could be berthing in Gothenbury Sunday afternoon. This would allow us time, after arrival, for a relaxed and smooth change from the working to social routine, a more than welcome luxury.

On entering the dining saloon for the evening meal, early sitting, it was very apparent that some of our passengers were determined not to waste any time in partaking of the chef's cuisine. That was not quite what the Catering Department had in mind but, as usual and undaunted, they simply dealt with the situation in a predictable manner. The second courses were politely delayed for an interminable period of time, with the galley being blamed for the delay.

Much to the chagrin of the passengers, we didn't experience any delay with our courses. The penny slowly dropping among them about not appearing prematurely before their mealtime gongs.

'Do you know anything about the Haga?' enquired one of the passengers sat at an adjacent table.

'Sorry, I didn't realise you were asking me,' I replied.

I thought the lady was talking to the Saloon Steward, who was serving nearby, but apparently the question had been directed at me. She was slightly tipsy and wasn't focussing, either aurally or visually. Here goes, I thought, just praying my words would not be misunderstood.

'To be honest, I know little about Gothenburg apart from the central shopping area and the Liseberg Amusement Park. The big department stores are Ferd Lundquist, Meeths, the Varuhuset Grand and Gillblads. They are all situated in the town centre,' I told her.

I don't think the good lady took the blindest bit of notice of the information I was giving her.

'Well I'm told it is an absolute gem. Right in the shen-shenture of the sh-shity,' she struggled on. 'I can't wait to see it,' she added.

I tried again. She was a lovely lady abandoned temporarily by her husband in his pursuit of more liquid refreshment.

'I have a tourist pamphlet of the place but I haven't got round to studying it yet. I've only recently joined the vessel. After the meal, I'll have a look at it and see if the Haga is mentioned then I'll let you know,' I added.

To my surprise, not only was the Haga mentioned but in some considerable detail. It looked as if the lady was well informed. My pamphlet described it as 'an old world city of wooden houses, the homes of Bohemians, students and artists, with picturesque shops offering antiques and many bargains.' All of this was apparently on our door step, almost.

I read on. If one looked inside the shops, the names would read 'Come and Look', 'Little London', 'Porto Bello Antique Shop', 'Inger Lises Antique Shop', 'Bengt in Haga', 'Boheme', 'The Bargain of the Day' and so on . . .

One could even learn to be a conjuror with Gothenburg's leading exponent, Jonnie Casino, in residence.

Rather than risk an embarrassing foray on the passenger deck, I handed the leaflet to the Stewardess to pass on, asking her to excuse my absence because of duty requirements. It now looked as if I had another place to visit if time permitted, but certainly not in preference to my first two choices.

'Third, we've quite a few items for Class Survey when we return to the UK so I want you and the Second to make sure that everything's OK with these items before we leave Gothenburg.'

The Chief's words brought me back to reality. It didn't look as if the opportunity to enjoy forays ashore during the day was on the agenda.

'OK Chief, whatever you say. I'll discuss a programme with the Second Engineer and deal with the work you require,' I replied.

As it turned out, there was still time to get a couple of nights ashore but any thoughts about visiting the Haga was definitely not on the agenda.

'You know, these Swedish girls are mouth-watering,' sighed the Second Mate as we sat in the Liseberg café bar the following evening. There was no doubt that, in their minds, we were fair game. They were light years ahead of their British counterparts when it came to matters of sex equality. As far as they were concerned, providing you were smartly dressed and were available, there was no harm in asking.

'Hi, you two sailors lonely?' enquired an amply proportioned, scantily clad young lady in perfect English. Her friends were not quite as attractive, slightly older and possibly of mixed breeding.

'Could it be, our luck has changed, Paul?' commented the Second Mate.

There was no doubt at all that his comment registered very positively with our new lady friends, judging by the way they were nodding heads frantically in the right direction and giggling profusely.

'We go downtown, if you like. Good bars, good fun,' persisted our blonde acquaintance.

'How much cash have you on you, Paul? It'll be bloody expensive with this crowd in tow.'

'I guess just about enough, provided they don't drink ruddy champagne,' I replied.

'OK, you're on,' he smiled to our blonde friend.

They lost no time in securing a taxi. We piled in, with bated breath, wondering just what fate had in store for us as we headed downtown.

24

'How much did it all cost then, Paul?' queried the Second Mate next day as we sat in the mess room drinking strong black cups of coffee, both of us feeling distinctly off colour.

Neither of us had much of a recollection of the night before. What the hell we had been drinking neither of us could remember, but whatever it was, it packed a dastardly punch, leaving one's head and stomach not exactly in harmony with one another.

'Well I'm cleaned out. I don't remember paying for the taxi back to the ship. Did you?' I replied.

'No, I certainly didn't. I guess our Swedish friends must have paid in advance, then. I reckon their evening was just nicely under way. Obviously they decided it was time to seek fresh conquests.'

'Some girls, eh? They certainly know what they're about and don't waste any time getting there, do they?'

'Guess not. But they do have safety in numbers. I reckon we were easy prey,' he added.

'I can promise you this. Next time I go ashore, it will be to the Ullevi Stadium, come hell or high water.'

And so it was. The following afternoon I set my sights and headed off in the general direction of the stadium with about 5 miles to cover on foot. At least it would allow me an opportunity to see a bit of the city that had passed unnoticed previously. Whether or not I would pass through the Haga remained to be seen. The area was not shown on the town centre map but I was able to confirm that the stadium was in the same direction as the Liseberg Park.

Walking the streets and crossing the roads in Gothenburg needed even more care than normal because of the trams that criss-crossed in all directions. This meant changing my direction several times. After a while, I had a feeling that maybe I was getting lost.

I decided to ask a passer-by. He obviously didn't get my meaning and turned to another passer-by for help. This young lady smiled and, after a brief conversation in Swedish, turned to me and asked in perfect English, 'Can I help you?'

'I'm trying to find the Ullevi Stadium. Am I heading in the right direction please?'

'You are, you are almost there. As I am going in that direction myself, you may wish to walk with me, if you like,' she offered.

'That is very kind of you,' I replied. 'I certainly will.'

It turned out she was a local girl and was heading off to work at the time. We chatted on; her command of English was magnificent. She even enquired whether I was married and where I lived. It turned out that she was hoping to visit the UK before too long. Probably we could meet again, she thought, if she sailed on one of the company's vessels. I gave her my name and the company's details, so that she could contact me if she wanted to.

'It is a shame you are not returning. I could have shown you around the city. There are four beautiful parks only about two kilometres from where we are now. Never mind, maybe one day we shall meet again.'

I thanked her for her help and we bid each other farewell outside the stadium. Once again, I thought, I always manage to meet a member of the opposite sex with promise, too late.

It turned out that visitors were welcome at the stadium, with guided tours during weekdays between June and August. It had only been built six years before and had a capacity of 50,000 spectators, mainly seated. It catered for football and athletics during summer and ice hockey, ice skating and ice speedway during winter. The facilities were truly outstanding, with restaurants and cafeteria areas, and it all seemed light years ahead of our own stadia.

I just hoped that sometime in the future, a return visit would be possible. The thought of seeing speedway bikes performing on ice made me wonder about the sanity of the riders taking part. When I passed on the information to those on board, there was a fair measure of doubt expressed about my sanity also.

'I take it you'll be wanted to venture ashore again tomorrow night then, Third,' suggested the Chief when I told him about my chance meeting ashore.

'I didn't even ask her, Chief. It's my duty night on board and presumably we'll be sailing the following evening. This has happened to me so many times, I'm losing count,' I added.

He didn't pursue the matter further.

I was beginning to think that Christine was still feeling aggrieved about our lack of contact with one another. I hadn't received a letter from her and that certainly didn't look promising at all. I was supposed to be driving south to see her at the end of the current voyage.

I had previously requested the company to release me from the vessel to enable me to continue my studies and, with tongue in cheek, asked for a fortnight's break before this, which very nicely coincided with our arrival back in the UK.

To my surprise and pleasure, the company agreed to my requests, so I decided this must be a good omen. I departed from the vessel in a reasonably optimistic mood, thinking that the current Beatles hit song 'I'm Feeling Glad All Over' was particularly appropriate in the circumstances.

'You're off again then, Paul? I hope you know what you're doing,' my mother commented as I packed my bags. She was not at all certain that pursuing a friendship with a girl in the south was a very clever idea at all.

'I'll just have to see what type of reception I get and take it from there. Anyway, Jennifer and family will be pleased to see me as usual,' I replied.

25

As I sped south, I knew no matter what reception I received from my girlfriend, my sister and her family would make the visit worthwhile. I certainly had no intention of changing course about trying to obtain full seagoing certification, and if that meant losing out with my girlfriend, so be it.

Imagine my surprise on reaching my sister's home to be greeted by Christine with a massive hug and a kiss to match.

'I've missed you so much, Paul. I just can't believe you're here at last. What's the matter, aren't you pleased to see me?'

Unfortunately, I've never been very good at hiding my reactions to unexpected circumstances. My first thought was, this can't be happening for real. My second was, did I remember to bring my gift for her from Sweden? I couldn't remember packing it. My final thought was, why had she apparently had a change of heart? No doubt all of those thoughts registered on my countenance.

'Of course I'm delighted to see you. I just thought you'd consiged me to the reject pile. Anyway, just to prove you've been in my thoughts, I've hopefully got a little something for you when I unpack my bags.'

That I was encouraged to do as soon as possible. Thankfully, I found what I was looking for.

'This is absolutely gorgeous! Aren't I lucky, Jennifer, having your brother as my number one boyfriend,' she added, turning to my sister, who nodded in agreement as she helped me to put it on her wrist.

'How long are you able to stay, Paul?' my sister enquired.

'Well, I'm due to start at college when it re-opens in ten days' time but I shall have to be back a couple of days before, to prepare. So I suppose I shall be here for a good week. Anyway, let's forget that, please. It's just great to be here again.'

As usual, my three-year-old niece jumped into my arms and tried to outdo my girlfriend in the big hug department.

Later that evening, as I glanced at the morning newspaper, the headlines reminded me of a previous unintentional encounter in a London Dockland pub: 'KRAY BROTHERS ARRESTED ON A MURDER CHARGE'. The tale that was to eventually unfold about these gents was certainly not in the fairytale category.

Fortunately, Christine was able to take a couple of days off work, but even then the time sped by and almost before it seemed I'd arrived, it was time to be heading back north.

'It's been really great, Paul. I really am going to miss you again. If I can get a week off work at your mid-term break, would it be all right if I come and stay at your home?' she asked.

'Now that seems a brilliant idea to me. I know my folks would love you to,' I replied.

My sister sensed the growing fondness between us but she did remind me that my girlfriend's mum was an extremely persuasive person so I shouldn't be too surprised if there were more twists and turns with our relationship in the future.

I was extremely reluctant to leave, knowing what faced me in the immediate future. On the journey, I tried to drown out my mixed feelings with large, loud helpings of the latest pop music on the car radio.

It didn't take long for me to be reminded that I had arrived home.

'I take it, I shall be getting my usual lift into the city,' my father enquired, shortly after my return.

Not only had he then only five minutes' walk to reach his

office, he also made a considerable saving in his travel expenses.

'Yes, mornings only, I assume,' I replied.

By then, he was working part-time, being well into his retirement, supposedly. He enjoyed spending time in his garden in the afternoon but was confined to the shed if rain stopped play.

The thought of returning to theoretical studies on subjects I had last dealt with seven years previously was not only daunting but extremely challenging. However, the college lecturers were well capable of getting their message over and it wasn't too long before I actually started to enjoy the study environment.

One of our lecturers, a young serious chap, took a fair degree of pleasure in testing our knowledge and verbal responses to his deep and penetrating questions. I did my best to avoid his attention as some of his more demanding theory left me grasping at straws.

Then, during one particular lecture, I thought my opportunity had finally come to demonstrate my knowledge about practical reality. He was lecturing on the theory of Simple Harmonic Motion and, looking around the class, he asked us to give him examples to illustrate the theory in addition to the ones he had mentioned himself.

There was a deafening silence from the gathered throng. Then a flash of inspiration unexpectedly struck me.

'Bed springs,' I proclaimed in a loud, sure and steady voice.

Heads swivelled like spinning tops.

'Now then, who, may I ask, suggested that?' our lecturer enquired.

I raised my hand.

'A very interesting suggestion, may I say. Please explain your thinking so we can all grasp the significance of what you mean. Please don't rush. We've all the time in the world,' he added.

Then the penny dropped, in all directions, so to speak. The titters grew louder by the second, followed by guffaws, then belly-aching squeals rent the air as handkerchiefs swept across faces, trying to stem watering eyes, with bodies rolling in all directions.

'Where has he disappeared to,' choked my colleague alongside, referring to our missing lecturer.

'Probably messed himself,' somebody called out from the front.

'You don't contribute much very often, Paul, but it's a killer when you do. How about continuing the lecture and showing us on the blackboard how your bed spring theory works out.'

This suggestion was greeted with unanimous approval by all present.

I pleaded that, as my artistic capability was strictly limited, it might be better if they used their imaginations to work out what I meant. After all, I didn't want to be accused of adorning the blackboard with obscene drawings.

Unfortunately, most of the study period was not a laughing matter. However, by some good fortune my memory recall of past studies coincided with the subjects under consideration, and consequently I felt a whole lot better for this small mercy.

26

'Only a week now until Christine arrives,' my mother reminded me as I arrived home one day from college.

'Don't I know it, Mum. As I shan't be doing any work while she's here, I'm trying to catch up with a load of theory we're supposed to complete then,' I replied.

I was longing to see Christine again. As her train drew into the station, with my heart racing in anticipation, I strained to find her among the milling crowd of passengers disembarking from the ten or so carriages.

'Hi, there,' I yelled as loud as I could, but that was as far as I managed.

'Some mothers do have 'em,' was one of the many cryptic comments that reached my ears as Christine enveloped me in her arms. Unfortunately she had caught me off balance, with the result that not only the two of us but also a few more of the less fortunate passengers landed on our backsides on the platform in what could only be described as a fully collapsed rugby scrum.

'Sorry, everyone, that was my fault,' cried Christine, with tears rolling down her cheeks.

That fooled everyone, including myself, until we realised like idiots that her tears were not of unhappiness; instead she was nearly wetting herself with laughter.

'How did the journey go, then?' I asked as we drove along the city street away from the railway station.

'Not as dramatic as the arrival, thank goodness, but OK, I suppose. Anyway, it's great to be here.'

How much my folks were expecting to see of her I hadn't

a clue, but in the ensuing week we were destined to travel to places far and wide in the area. We visited the Yorkshire Dales, the Moors, the Wolds, the main coastal resorts and, last but not least, the Spurn Peninsula, which extends down from the Plain of Holderness into the Humber Estuary for over a mile.

My relatively new car attracted a fair bit of attention but this was more than probably due to the very attractive female alongside me.

'Paul, there is just one place we haven't been to which has always mystified me ever since I read *Jane Eyre* a few years ago,' she mentioned one evening as we sat in the local pub enjoying a drink.

'That must be Brontë country,' I replied. 'We were only about twenty miles away from there the other day. If I'd known, we could easily have made the detour.'

'Well, next time I come north to see you, we could go then,' she suggested.

'Sure thing, although, to be honest, it is pretty bleak and uninviting in the immediate area up there on the top of the Pennines so it's best to choose a good day, weatherwise,' I replied.

I remembered a childhood visit with my family many years previously to Haworth and the famous parsonage when we lived not all that far away. There was such an inexplicable sense of remoteness about the buildings despite their now being located in a partly built-up area that a feeling of foreboding had remained in my thoughts ever since.

It was Christine's first visit north ever and I was interested, naturally enough to discover what she considered to be the best features.

'If you don't mind my saying, Paul, that is a daft question to ask. I wouldn't have come at all if you hadn't been here. Anyway, apart from you, what can I say? I still haven't got over the remoteness of the Dales or the grandeur of the Moors nor, for that matter, the majesty of the coastline.

Those cliffs at Bempton are fantastic and so is the Flamborough Headland with those cavernous caves,' she added.

'I do hope Paul isn't running you off your feet with all this gadding about the countryside, Christine,' my mother remarked one day just before the end of her stay.

'Heavens no, it's been absolutely great. I had no idea at all that this part of the country was so attractive and interesting. Paul has taken me just about everywhere worth seeing, I think,' she replied. 'I just hope he manages to pass his examinations and gets put on a ship sailing from London again,' she added.

I promised her that I would do everything in my power to realise these aspirations as we said our fond farewells and I waved her goodbye.

Although they didn't say so much, I guessed my parents both thought that I was pushing my luck no end in pursuing my friendship with a girl so far distant from my home, particularly with such long intervals of time between our meetings. Nevertheless, a grim determination to succeed with the examinations, drove me along at a fast and furious rate of knots.

'How did they go then, Paul,' asked Christine, after I had completed the saga.

'Let's say I'm hopeful. They weren't as bad as I'd expected,' I replied. 'I should have the results soon and I'm reporting back into the office tomorrow, so keep your fingers crossed,' I added.

It was coming up to Christmas 1965. My exam results would be released soon afterwards and the company decided that I should remain available locally for relief work for the time being.

Once again, I was wishing that circumstances could be a whole lot different but, from a practical standpoint, there was no way that I could intervene to alter things.

'Congratulations, Third, you certainly tried hard and deserve to have passed.'

Our Superintendent Engineer was obviously pleased with my success.

'I'm looking at our manning arrangements at the present time. I am right in thinking you would prefer to sail out of London again, for personal reasons?' he enquired.

'You certainly are, sir. My girlfriend is from Kent so that would suit me fine. Hopefully I would then be able to see quite a bit more of her,' I replied.

'Right, leave it with me. You may have to do some London vessel-relieving as Second Engineer at first, but I am pretty sure you won't have any complaints about that.'

I couldn't wait to pass on the good news to Christine, who was actually beginning to believe that the life of a seafarer was not always bad news. Whether or not her mother would ever accept that, only time would tell.

'Welcome on board the *Virgo*, Second.' The Chief Engineer's words took me by surprise as I boarded the vessel in London, my promotion having temporarily slipped my memory.

Although I would not be sailing on this good vessel, I was anxious to establish an involvement with those on board in my new role. Probably the most important factor for me was to achieve an effective working relationship with those providing services to the vessel in port, particularly the repair personnel. After all, money was being spent by the company to sort out problems sooner rather than later. I hadn't previously sailed on this class of vessel but from an engineering point of view that didn't present any difficulties.

The fact that I knew that I would not be sailing in the near future meant that I had taken my car down to London, so when the weekend arrived, I exercised the privilege of my new position and took off to see my girlfriend, leaving the lower ranks to look after things.

'Paul, I wouldn't mind coming back tomorrow with you to see the ship. We could also have a look at James Bond's Aston Martin, which is being stored in a garage my uncle's friend owns. It's the car that was used in the *Goldfinger* film,' Christine exclaimed.

'OK, although the vessel is no great shakes. I'll take you back to town tomorrow provided you don't mind going back home on the train tomorrow night,' I said.

She didn't, thank goodness, because I was more than curious to find out how her uncle's friend came to be providing a roof over that famous car.

27

We were moored in the Pool of London almost at Tower Bridge. The wharf was located in no man's land on the south bank of the River Thames.

'Paul, this is really a creepy place. I wouldn't like to be walking along this street on a dark and windy night,' exclaimed Christine.

'You're seeing this on a Sunday morning with everything quiet and peaceful. Yes, I suppose it does look a bit sinister, but come tomorrow morning it will be a hive of activity and you wouldn't think twice about feeling safe in this area,' I replied.

She wasn't all that impressed with the vessel, one which had been built immediately after the war. There didn't seem much point in hanging about on board.

'Where's this famous car parked then, Christine? I can't wait to get a close-up look and see what all the fuss is about.'

'Well, my uncle's friend lives in Chelsea and does art work for the film industry. I gather he converted one of his rooms into a garage, otherwise he'd have had nowhere to park. During filming the car was driven to locations in the London area from a garage on the North Circular Road. The trouble was, drivers were recognising it and then trying to demonstrate their cars were easily capable of seeing off the Aston Martin. That, naturally, didn't go down at all well with the police. Apparently, that's when my uncle's friend stepped in with his offer to provide a roof over its head at his house and the film people accepted.'

'I wouldn't be at all surprised if he isn't making a killing,' I replied. 'I hope he's told his insurers, otherwise they might want to do the killing,' I added.

We set off in the general direction of Chelsea, crossing the river at Tower Bridge, and in what seemed no time at all we'd arrived at our destination – but then it was a Sunday.

Our host was pleased to greet us but could barely conceal his amusement when he told us that the famous car was not there but was actually on public exhibition that day in the Battersea Park pleasure grounds. As there was nowhere to park immediately in Chelsea, we thanked our host for his help, excused ourselves and set off once again back across the river to Battersea.

'Would you credit that, Christine? I suppose we should have checked first.'

Already there were masses of people heading in the general direction and I feared the worst but managed to squeeze into a parking place only a stone's throw from the park entrance.

They say seeing is believing but the car literally took one's breath away. Even the Walther PK was lying on top of the dash board, but unloaded, thankfully.

'It barely seems credible that all these buttons and levers work,' I said, pointing to the mass of gadgetry laid out in front of us.

'Surely this car won't go into mass production? It would be more like one of the old Chicago gangland movies if the crooks in this city managed to get their hands on them.'

'You're dead right there, Christine. Sorry about the pun. Seriously though, these buttons here fire the front machine-guns, these levers operate the tyre cutters that look like the wheel hubcaps. Then there are the defence systems. This switch operates the rear bulletproof screen, these buttons operate the smokescreens and it looks as if these switches are for the oil slicks.'

'It must have cost a fortune. Apart from the publicity for them, I wonder why Aston Martin wanted to develop a car

126

like this? It isn't as if they would be allowed to market them, would they?'

'No, my love, hardly – particularly as the passenger seat you're occupying can be ejected by pressing this button on top of the gear knob. Don't panic, though, I'm not going to see if it works,' I added.

'Paul, let's get someone to take our photograph while we're sat in the car,' suggested Christine.

One of the security staff duly obliged with my camera and we just hoped that he had managed to capture our moment of glory sitting in this magnificent vehicle. He reckoned that the real reason for the car being moved from its previous location was the persistent hassle that inteprid souvenir hunters were causing for the garage security staff, who were fed up to their back teeth trying to prevent the loss of vital parts.

The day sped by. My efforts to reach Victoria Station in time for Christine to catch her train only just proved successful with barely time to say goodbye.

'I'll telephone you tomorrow night,' I shouted as loudly as possible as the train accelerated into the distance. I doubted if she caught a single word of my message.

'Second, there's a message from the Superintendent's office for you. They want you to relieve on the *Draco*, which is due to arrive in London the day after this vessel sails.'

The Chief Engineer greeted me with the good news shortly after my return from the railway station.

'That's fine by me, Chief. I won't give you a prize for guessing who will be more than a little pleased with that news,' I replied.

I just prayed and hoped that things would soon sort themselves out with a vessel for me to sail on out of London, to help my chances of continuing my relationship with my girlfriend. I was tempted to make some enquiries of our Superintendent's office but as it didn't seem to matter that one's private affairs counted for a great deal in the general scheme of things, I decided to let sleeping dogs lie, at least for the immediate future.

'Hi there, it's Paul. I've got some good news, Christine. I'm staying in London for the time being and relieving on the next vessel due in a couple of days,' I told her next evening when I rang her.

'Oh, that's great. Can I come up to see you again?' she enquired.

'I would hope so, my love, but a lot depends on the Chief Engineer. I'm not sure whether he lives in the south or not. If he doesn't and there's no chief to relieve him, I shan't be able to get away, so you would have to come up by train next time as well,' I replied.

'As long as you promise to meet me at Victoria Station, I don't mind at all coming up to town on the train,' she said.

We left it at that and hoped for the best.

As it turned out, the *Draco* was ahead of schedule and arrived in London before the *Virgo* sailed, which did not help at all. Obviously, I couldn't be in two places at the same time yet my services were required on both vessels.

Fortunately the Chief Engineer on the *Virgo* appreciated my predicament and released me, and in no time I had driven downriver to the *Draco's* berth.

The greeting extended to me was far from welcoming.

'Where the hell did you get to, Second? I've been sat here all morning waiting for you to turn up. The relief chief isn't arriving until tomorrow. I was told you would be waiting to board the vessel as we berthed, so I phoned my wife to let her know I would be on my way home three hours ago. She'll wonder where on earth I am,' he said in dismay.

'I'm terribly sorry, Chief, but this situation isn't of my making. I've come here straight from the *Virgo*, as soon as the Chief released me. If you can quickly run over your repair and store requisition lists with me, you can then get away,' I suggested.

He eventually accepted that I had been the victim of circumstances beyond my control but he was still fuming about his delayed departure.

Had I any inkling of the relief Chief's impish nature and his rather warped sense of humour, I wouldn't have encouraged my girlfriend to venture up to town yet again. I still had a lot to learn.

28

'When are we going to meet her then, Second?' enquired the relief Chief the following day. I knew from previous spells of relieving with him that he was a character and a half, particularly when it came to entertaining the opposite sex in port. According to those who had sailed with him, there was never a dull moment whilst he was around and woe betide anyone who thought a quiet life might be possible if one chose to remain on board in port.

'Well, Chief, if you've no objection, she could travel up for the weekend, but that's all, because she has to be back at work on Monday morning,' I replied.

'Fair enough. I'll look forward to that. I'll make sure my hospitality is up to the mark. And you make sure the Chief Steward is aware, then he'll have a passenger cabin available for her,' he added.

'The sailing Chief was not at all impressed with my late arrival, I'm afraid,' I said, changing subjects quickly. 'Anyway, as you can see, he hasn't much in the way of repairs to be dealt with. Just the usual boiler cleaning and the starboard boiler for Lloyds Survey.'

'The trouble with this bloody company is that they expect one to be mind readers, Second. Half the time they just expect you to anticipate their intentions,' he replied.

It soon became obvious that having the availability of my car at the ship meant that I was considered a quick fix for immediate travel problems. Not only that, the relief Chief decided that I was an ideal chauffeur for evening trips to his favourite watering holes, and whilst he didn't expect me to buy his drinks, I contributed the rest.

On the other hand, having your girlfriend stay on board in port was not usual at that time. Most of the captains and chief stewards ruled such a practice out of the question, but nobody challenged the relief Chief on these matters, so I had something to be grateful for.

I certainly had a few misgivings about his ideas on hospitality but, as far as I was concerned, the weekend couldn't arrive quickly enough, in any event.

'Right on time again, Christine. Southern Region certainly know how to keep their trains on time,' I commented, as I greeted her on the Friday evening at Victoria Station.

'I'm absolutely ravenous, Paul. I didn't have time to get anything to eat before I caught the train. Can we grab a takeaway on the way back to the vessel, please?' she asked.

'Sure thing. In fact, I'm feeling decidedly peckish myself,' I responded.

After purchasing our usual Chinese fare at the local establishment, as we headed back towards the vessel, I felt it might be a good idea to mention to Christine that the Chief's hospitality might prove just a little unusual in her experience.

'Paul, I might be younger than you, but don't forget I've lived abroad most of my life. Some of the hospitality I've come across would make your eyes pop open. I am not the slightest bit concerned about anything he may come up with,' she assured me with a beguiling wink. 'After all, I've got you to protect me from his advances,' she smiled.

'He won't be trying that on, I'm certain, but he has a wicked sense of humour, so be warned,' I replied.

As it turned out, the relief Chief had accepted an invitation to join the Mate and some of his London friends ashore, so all was relatively calm as we boarded the vessel. After the Chief Steward showed her the cabin for her stay, we demolished our takeaways with murderous intent.

'Paul, I don't know whether I should mention this or not. My mum wasn't at all pleased about me coming up again this weekend. Apparently she was expecting me to look after my sister. I'm afraid we had a bit of a row. In fact, it was more than that. I'm not sure whether she had any plans at all, quite honestly. I just don't think she wanted me to come, really,' she added.

'I must admit I don't like the sound of that. Maybe your mum is just concerned about your safety, but probably there's more to it than that,' I suggested. 'Don't you think you should telephone her and let her know that you've arrived safely?'

We decided to leave well alone. Her mother would more than likely only upset the apple cart and I was not in a position to do much to alleviate the situation.

'Let's get ourselves a drink and forget your dear mum, Christine,' I suggested after we had finished our takeaways.

We returned to my cabin and were just getting comfy and cosy when the unmistakable tones of the relief Chief resounded down the lower deck alleyway. He sounded to be in good form and was obviously accompanied by at least two females. Then the Mate's dulcet tones manifested themselves just as clearly. I pressed my fingers onto Christine's lips and waited to see where they were heading. The voices grew louder and the Chief's cabin door was thrown open with a loud clatter. Seconds later, music reverberated in wild abandon, drowning out the verbal exchanges from the cabin next door.

'Are you going to let him know you're back?' whispered Christine.

'That's up to you, my love. Don't hold me responsible for the consequences. Knowing the Chief, he'll have you performing before his guests.' I warned. The fact that he wasn't aware she had a good singing voice would not remain a secret for long, for sure.

'Sorry, Paul. I can't wait to meet him and his guests. I bet you he doesn't get me singing,' she claimed.

'Be it on your head. You've been warned. I haven't a

132

clue who the females are. Probably a couple of the local call girls. Anyway, stay here, I'll see what his reaction is.'

I knocked on his cabin door. 'It's only me, Chief. Can I come in?' I asked.

'Thought you were ashore, Second. Course you can come in. Allow me to introduce you to the Mate's sister and her friend,' he replied.

The usual pleasantries were exchanged. I was trying to decide whether the Chief was having me on. I was aware the Chief Officer was a southerner but I wouldn't put it past him to kid me about the females.

'Just a moment, Second. What's happened about your girlfriend,' the Chief urgently enquired.

'She's sat in my cabin, awaiting your invitation,' I replied, trying to sound as if I was kidding him.

'You're not joking, Second, for goodness' sake? Show her in, you silly sod, before I boot you up your backside,' he threatened.

The remainder of the evening remains a pleasant blur on my memory. I distinctly remember his extremely gracious welcome to Christine, his capacity to offer almost anything in the way of liquid refreshment to his guests and, last but not least, his determination to provide plenty of entertainment, whether that be anecdotes, jokes or music.

It was only after awakening the following morning on my settee, fully dressed, that I panicked about what had happened to Christine.

I appeared at her cabin in no time, only to discover her door locked. I glanced at my watch and headed for the dining saloon to find her sitting alongside the Chief Engineer at the Captain's table.

'Morning, Second. Aren't you joining us for breakfast?' he enquired.

'Er, no, I don't think so, thank you, Chief. I'll see you after breakfast, Christine,' I replied.

My concern about her welfare, coupled with my churning insides, had temporarily killed my appetite.

'You missed a super breakfast, Paul.' She was obviously impervious to the Chief's hospitality.

'Whatever happened last night, Christine? I barely remember the proceedings. How did it go, then?'

'Absolutely hilarious. Surely you remember the Chief's joke about the chimps and the tea party?' she queried.

'Vaguely, I'm afraid. You'll have to remind sometime. Did you sleep OK?'

'Yes, but I missed you. You were not really in a loving mood last night, you know,' she said.

'What can I say but sorry? I always manage to sabotage myself,' I replied.

I was forgiven, at least by the time we were parted once again. I just hoped that she could patch things up with her mother when she arrived home.

29

Just when I was beginning to think that my chance of joining a vessel sailing from London had passed me by, matters came to a head out of the blue.

'Second, the Superintendent is in my cabin and he has some good news for you. Can you come up right away?' enquired the Chief on the telephone to the engine room.

'We want you to join the *Aries* as Second Engineer when this vessel arrives here at the end of the week. You had better return north today and get your sailing gear together and then return on Friday. OK, Second?' asked the superintendent.

'Most certainly, sir. Absolutely great, couldn't be better. I'm very grateful,' I replied.

I knew that the *Aries* was on a fortnightly service between London and east Sweden and I couldn't have asked for a better service from all points of view. Naturally, I wanted to tell Christine the good news but that would have to wait for the moment.

As I drove home, I couldn't help but reflect, once again, on the twists and turns of a seafarer's way of life. I would also have to decide whether to return to London in my car, provided I could leave it in the south safely while I was away.

I couldn't help but detect some sense of misgiving when I passed on my news to my parents.

'I just hope it all works out well for you, Paul. It doesn't look as if we shall be seeing much of you in the future, though,' my father commented.

'Knowing our Paul, he'll keep showing up, just like he does at his sister's in Kent,' my mother added.,

'That's more than likely, Mum. But it will all depend on whether I'm ever relieved while the vessel is in London. I don't think the company have given me a London-based vessel just out of the goodness of their hearts. I know they don't relieve the chief engineers who live within around fifty miles of London. They expect them to travel each day between home and London. So they may have the same idea in mind for me. Who knows? After all, they know I have a roof over my head in Kent whenever I need one.'

Just as I expected, my girlfriend was over the moon when I told her the news.

'Fantastic, Paul. Ring me as soon as you're back in London, won't you,' she demanded.

I promised her that I would do that very thing.

I was in two minds what to do about travelling back but in the end chose the train, just in case I didn't have time to get suitable garaging sorted out for my car before we sailed.

I joined the *Aries* in the Millwall Dock the day after the vessel berthed, to find that the previous second engineer had already departed to go on leave but the Chief, whose home was also in Kent, quickly put my mind at ease regarding any immediate problems that might need sorting out.

'The last Second was a good lad. He knew this was your first sailing trip as Second so he's dealt with all the shore personnel matters. There just maybe a need to replace one of our ratings if he can't get some marital problems sorted out. The shipping office is not far away if you have to obtain a replacement crew member, but that will be no problem whatsoever,' the Chief added.

It was only when I stepped into the engine room for the first time that I began to comprehend what it meant to be sailing on a choice vessel. Apparently a No. 1 choice for the London pool of seafarers, for reasons which would soon become very clear to me and probably why one of our ratings was having marital problems. The engine room was spotless. You could eat a meal off the floor plates, almost.

I soon struck up a good working relationship with the Chief. He was direct, down to earth, with no hassle at all.

'Look, Second, all you have got to do is ask the ratings to do what you need done. You don't have to force the issue at all, just make it abundantly clear what your orders are. OK?' the Chief told me before we sailed.

This plan of action was breaking new ground for me. I'd been used to trusting virtually no one, particularly if lives were at risk. You only ended up carrying the can if things went wrong. Anyway, I took the Chief's advice and, sure enough, as if by magic and with no fuss at all, orders were carried out in a relaxed and efficient manner with unbelievable co-operation from all concerned.

I was even able to keep well on top of the paperwork which was a necessary evil that accompanied the rank I had attained. It almost seemed as if there must be some financial inducement on offer to the ratings, such was their eagerness to please.

The Chief kept himself well occupied with an abundance of typing which was never visible when one was in his cabin. Curiosity got the better of me one day.

'You certainly have a lot of work to do on your typewriter, Chief. Must be wearing your finger tips to the bone,' I suggested.

'Not really, Second. I'm just working on some papers, nothing too serious,' he winked.

I pondered whether he was earning some ill-gotten gains from his efforts, like others I had come across in my travels. He quickly changed the subject.

'By the way, Second, I nearly forgot to remind you that this Sunday's inspection will almost certainly be a little different to what you will have come across in the past,' he warned. 'You will be somewhat surprised by the condition of the crew cabins. Don't make any comments, though, during the inspection. Just accept what you see as normal. OK?'

'No problem, Chief. I can't wait to see what it's all about,' I replied.

'One other thing, Second. You may be aware of an unusual flurry of activity in various parts of the vessel. Just ignore this and all will be well, I can assure you,' he advised.

I was totally at a loss to understand what the Chief was referring to.

We berthed in Norrkoping, our first port, but after only a few hours' stay, we were on passage to Stockholm. Sunday morning arrived during this passage and immediately after breakfast, the Captain called our attention to his inspection.

'Right, let's get to it. I will be proceeding in the usual order. Passenger, officers, midship crew accommodation and Catering Department, then finally the aft crew accommodation,' he explained.

The inspection did not include the bridge, radio room or the engine room and machinery compartments.

I was beginning to think the Chief had well and truly exaggerated the situation as we progressed around the accommodation spaces.

'Right, gentleman, let's proceed aft and complete our business,' the Old Man exclaimed.

As we entered the aft deck house, the first thing that struck me was the unusual aroma that pervaded one's nostrils, more akin to a boudoir than seamens' quarters. Then there was that distinct *clip-clop* of heels fading into the distance accompanied by a distinct girlish giggle or two. I daren't look at the other officers but there was not a glimmer on the Old Man's face.

We entered the PO's cabin. I just stared in astonishment at the pink wallpaper and matching carpet. The rest of the cabins were equally as well decorated; all were in absolutely immaculate condition, as were the bathrooms and showers, wash basins and toilets.

'Excellent,' said the Captain. 'Don't we maintain impressive standards on this vessel, Second?'

'I've never seen such standards before, sir,' I replied. I was still shell-shocked as we departed but the truth was slowly dawning on me.

After we had finished, I tackled the Chief right away.

'Who are the females and where did they disappear to?' I enquired.

'For heaven's sake, Second, use your head. They join the vessel at Norrkoping every trip. Think, where is the only place they could have gone to?' he asked.

'You mean, down the tunnel escape and the propeller shaft tunnel, into the engine room?'

'Now there's a clever Second Engineer,' replied the Chief. 'These females have been doing that ever since this vessel's been on this run, and what's more, they have never been caught, would you believe. They remain on board until we return to Norrkoping before we leave the Swedish coast. We never have any trouble with the crew, the passengers aren't even aware and, as you have seen, they keep the seamens' accommodation like a four-star hotel.'

30

Whilst it was becoming increasingly clear that our unofficial crew members ensured that exceptionally high standards of service were maintained by the remainder, it was only later in the voyage that another facet of their presence revealed itself.

Before that, an opportunity to see a little of Stockholm presented itself somewhat unexpectedly when our Agent boarded the vessel shortly after our arrival and requested some technical assistance.

The Chief Engineer suggested I accompany the Agent to his office and try to sort out a query which had come from another vessel on its way to Stockholm.

I had not expected to see such a grand vista as our taxi headed out through the city to our destination, a vista that included superb buildings, bridges and beautiful terrain which ranged itself in a truly breathtaking manner.

Thankfully, I was able to sort out the technical query relatively quickly so, on the return trip, I decided to dispense with the taxi and take a look around the city centre.

I suppose the splendour and scale of the department stores should not have surprised me but, once again, the affluence of the Swedish people as a whole was driven home to me by the abundance of high-quality and expensive goods on display. Certainly a Woolworths store, even a Marks and Spencers, would struggle not to look downmarket. Any thoughts of springing another surprise on my girlfriend, giftwise, soon got pushed into the recesses of my mind.

Our departure from Stockholm was eagerly awaited by

our additional crew members as they knew that we were then heading north up the Baltic Sea towards Gavle, which meant that our numbers would increase once again, albeit only temporarily.

'Second, we'll be having our usual safe arrival party in the Second Mate's cabin. You're very welcome,' the Third Mate advised me after we had berthed.

I gratefully accepted the invitation, blissfully unaware of what was in store that evening.

'Judging by the expression on your face, Paul, you must have just won the football pools,' exclaimed the Second Mate as I entered his cabin, to be confronted by an entire bevy of stunners wearing the briefest of skirts and little else. The sheer expanse of female flesh, lingering alluring looks and lightly furrowed and questioning brows, coupled with enticing perfumes, almost stopped my heart.

'Grab yourself a bottle, for heaven's sake, then we can get started,' he continued unabashed.

'You like poker, Paul?' enquired the closest female.

'Sure thing, I'm an absolute expert,' I lied.

'That's not fair,' she pouted. 'It's no fun if you do not lose. I shall sit on your knee,' she decided, parking her warm bum firmly in position.

Quite what effect she thought that would have on the outcome I couldn't imagine, but for certain I was going to have to try to avoid losing, otherwise my embarrassment would know no bounds.

'She's got a point or two there, Paul,' commented the Second Mate, trying to keep his face straight. 'Anyway, it's all above board, on the table and anywhere else you may want it,' he added for good measure.

Poker was a card game that I, in keeping with most seafarers, had played on numerous previous occasions, sometimes with fairly spectacular losses mainly due to lack of concentration and loss of memory.

'Right, Ulrika, what are you forfeiting?' asked the Second Mate.

My attention strayed, not for the first time, chiefly

141

because of my close encounters with the dear lady. Suddenly, without warning, she jumped off my knee and shed her skirt, leaving her with just a G string and her flimsy top. It was certainly a case of in for a penny, in for a pound – maybe even a krona or two.

Her brave actions were duly applauded in the time-honoured fashion and she gracefully acknowledged our appreciation of her efforts to please us. I couldn't help but feel a trifle guilty about enjoying the entertainment; after all, I had turned up wearing not just belt and braces but a few more layers of clothing than normal.

Just as it was beginning to look as if we guys were in for a treat, the girls decided that fair play was not being exercised by the dealer.

'Are you accusing me of fiddling the cards,' asked the Second Mate.

Heads nodded in unison, in reply.

'I guess I had better plead guilty without further ado,' he volunteered.

'I reckon his crime is unforgivable, girls. There can only be one forfeit for that,' I replied.

'To a chorus of 'Strip now, not later', the Second Mate duly obliged, to loud cheers, screams of laughter and thunderous applause, then quickly disaappeared into the bathroom and didn't reappear.

Our return voyage to Norrkoping passed all too quickly, lacking in particular the party atmosphere. There was little cargo to load and following the disembarkation of our unofficial crew, we proceeded back to London in almost an automatic mode of operation, with words of command almost meaningless.

I had already decided to return home to collect my car regardless of possible garaging problems because my sister had volunteered to relinguish her garage space at home if I needed it. I had also promised the Chief Engineer I would return the following day without delay.

In view of the fact that my new car was fully run-in and the need not to delay my return, I decided to open up the car and get a feel of its true performance. This was, of course, before the 70 m.p.h. speed limit existed and the ideal place for such testing at that time was the A1.

After negotiating a roundabout and shortly after reaching 90 m.p.h, I was overtaken by a police car which was travelling only slightly faster. I decided to maintain my speed but maintain a respectable distance from the police car. We had travelled over 30 miles in this formation before reaching Huntingdon, where it was necessary to reduce speed to 30 m.p.h. I had just passed the speed limit signs when, to my surprise, the POLICE STOP sign lit up in the rear window of the car I was following. My heart missed a beat then sank in the direction of my stomach. I stopped close behind the police car then sat and waited, racking my brains as to why I had been stopped.

The two officers sauntered over as I wound down my window.

'Stop your engine, sir. Have you your licence and insurance certificate?' I was asked.

I handed them over and again awaited my fate with trepidation.

'Where are you travelling to, sir?' I was asked.

'Kent, in fact, to see my girlfriend. I've been away at sea for months.' I volunteered, then almost immediately wished I hadn't said that.

'Really, sir. It doesn't look as if you intend keeping her waiting too long,' the officer suggested.

So it was speeding – but where? I didn't understand at all.

'Don't look so worried, sir. We haven't stopped you to book you. Just to offer you some advice on your driving. First of all, when negotiating roundabouts, you should maintain the same lane if you intend to continue in the same general direction. Don't change lanes even if there is no other traffic about. Next, there is no need to keep returning to the nearside lane if you are travelling in continuous traffic at speeds over 70 m.p.h. Otherwise, we consider your driving is commendable. Keep it up and have a safe journey. Cheerio,' he concluded.

They drove off, leaving me in a stupor, amazed by the turn of the events. Never in my life did I expect to be stopped by traffic police for reasons other than law-breaking. The memory of those events is as vivid today as on the day they occurred.

31

Having brought my car down to London, I couldn't wait to seize the opportunity to travel down the A2 to see my family and girlfriend. In almost typical fashion, other events interceded.

'Paul, can you help me, please?' enquired the Second Mate. He wanted some information about one of the ratings in my department.

'Can't it wait until tomorrow, Dave? I'd like to beat the traffic exodus if possible, otherwise it will be the usual slow crawl out of town,' I replied.

'Sorry, I need the information for the shipping office first thing in the morning.'

'OK, give me five minutes, please, and I'll be along to see you,' I told him.

I trawled through my paperwork, found what was wanted and for no good reason at all, tried to run down the alleyway to the Second Mate's cabin. I didn't get very far. My head struck a pipe flange projecting down from the deckhead which I had walked past on numerous previous occasions with no trouble at all. I shuddered to a standstill with a million stars flashing in my eyes, then I sank to my knees in a flash. I struggled to my feet and continued to his cabin with blood pouring out of the top of my head.

'I just don't believe this, Dave. Can you stop the bleeding?' I pleaded.

'I'll try a spray that's supposed to do that, but I can't do much about your headache. You'll have to dose yourself up on codeine,' he suggested.

I thanked him profusely for his efforts. The bleeding had stopped and, apart from having a thumping headache, I soon recovered my equilibrium and was speeding on my way.

'Hi, Christine. Lovely to see you again. I've made a special effort to see you tonight, my love,' I groaned meaningfully, shortly after arriving at her home.

'You say that with an awful lot of feeling. Hold me tight and tell me why,' she whispered in my ear.

'Oh, you know. Missed you a lot. It always seems an eternity between my visits,' I explained. 'Come on, let's get rolling,' I continued. 'I just can't wait to get a pint of best British bitter at that pub at Fordwich.'

Christine was in a merry mood, making it quite difficult for me to concentrate on my driving. I just hoped I wasn't going to be stopped for erratic control of the car.

'What's it to be, then, my love?' I asked as we entered the pub lounge.

'Just the usual,' she replied.

We chatted, shared our secrets, had a few more drinks. It was a friendly, warm atmosphere and I was beginning to feel a lot better. Then almost without warning, the atmosphere changed. I glanced around the room. Several people were looking at me in very strange ways.

'Hey, what the hell is going on? People are looking at me as if I've grown horns,' I exclaimed.

She stopped gazing into my eyes, looked up and gasped.

'Paul, I don't believe it,' she murmured in disbelief.

'What, my love? What's the matter?' I pleaded.

'There's blood trickling down in rivulets from your scalp, all the way round your head. I've never seen anything like it in my life,' she struggled to say.

'Oh, hell, no.' I rushed into the gents' toilet and nearly fainted as I glanced in the mirror. Frankenstein's monster had truly arrived, or so it must have seen to those sitting near me in the lounge.

The publican joined me in the toilet. 'What's your game,

young man?' he enquired. 'Your friend out there is in a right state.'

I quickly recounted the earlier events that day and my accident on the vessel.

'Your problem now is that the alcohol has thinned your blood. I'll clean up your scalp and use a strong plaster. Then I'll inform her that you're OK,' he added.

I thanked him for his kindness and help and promised that I would go to the hospital in the morning. I then returned to the lounge and rejoined Christine.

I tried to smile at the gathered throng and promptly regretted it. It must have seemed to them that I was some kind of sick-minded joker.

I sat down at our table and explained what actually happened on board the vessel that afternoon.

'Are you sure you're OK?' my girlfriend asked in an extremely worried way.

'Yes, apart from a stinking rotten headache, but even that is wearing off now,' I replied.

'You were silly, Paul. You shouldn't have come down tonight, you know,' she whispered.

'Well, you know me.'

'Come on, let's drink up and be on our way. I know what will make you feel a lot better, and it doesn't come out of a bottle,' she winked.

Next morning, on my way back to London, I reflected on my wise decision to travel to Kent to see the girl in my life and in doing so, clean forgot to go to the hospital for medical attention.

I had scarcely boarded the vessel when the Second Mate grabbed me.

'Paul, I bet you haven't been to the Seamens' Hospital at Greenwich?' he enquired. 'You passed it on your way back, you know. It's only a couple of minutes down the road by car,' he added.

'Hell, no, completely forgot, Dave. I'll have a quick word

with the Chief Engineer then I'll go and suffer my fate at the hands of the hospital nurses,' I responded.

I followed the signs and found the receptionist. I explained to her what had happened on board the previous day and received an immediate ticking-off for not appearing sooner.

'Come this way, Mr James. Dr Charlton will see you shortly but, in order to save time, please remove all your clothes, apart from your underwear, in the cubicle over there then wait on the examination couch,' she ordered.

I did as requested and lay on the couch as that seemed the obvious thing to do.

'I take it you are Paul James then?' the Doctor enquired.

I woke with a start. 'Eh, oh, yes, that's right, doctor,' I stammered.

'Well, then, will you please make yourself decent, before we proceed,' was the next request.

I gazed up into the most beautiful blue eyes, glamorously gorgeous facial features and blindingly blonde hair vying with an equally blinding white coat.

' I maybe a doctor, Mr James, but I do have feelings,' she politely pointed out.

My embarrassment was overpowering, too uncomfortable to be true. I rolled over onto my tummy and prayed for the couch to swallow me up.

I will never wear briefs again, I murmured to myself.

'I'll return in a few minutes,' she stated. 'Hopefully, we can then proceed in a normal manner.'

After undergoing just about every conceivable test imaginable, I was pronounced fit for light duties. I was also given a severe dressing-down yet again.

'Do remember, Mr James, that concussion can have very serious consequences if the correct action isn't taken without delay. You certainly should not have been driving a motor vehicle in the state you were, you know, at least not until you had received a full check-up,' she added.

I wondered what she would have said if she had known

that driving was not the only matter I had been occupied with the previous evening.

'I've also given you an anti-tetanus booster as a precaution, and do not remove the dressing on your head for at least four days. It's protecting a plastic skin that I've applied. That wound should have been stitched after the accident and you are extremely lucky not to have suffered worse consequences,' I was admonished.

I thanked her profusely for her kind attention and apologised profusely for causing her embarrassment.

No one on board believed my story after I returned to the vessel.

32

Even before we sailed from London on our next voyage, rumours were spreading about the possibility of a national seamen's strike. It was increasingly obvious to us all that as the demands of most of the unions were being conceded by the employers at that time with a view to preventing further strikes, it would not be long before the National Union of Seamen was jumping on the same band-wagon. However, the attitude of the shipowning fraternity was not as accommodating as the manufacturing and shore service industries when it came to giving in to such pressures. Like many others, I feared the worst and just hoped and prayed that a strike wouldn't occur. Merchant Navy officers generally were members of the Merchant Navy and Airline Officers Association, which at that time operated entirely separately with regard to negotiating pay and conditions of service for their members. Nevertheless, they did feel that the Seamen's Union had many valid matters to try to resolve on behalf of their members.

We had only been at sea for a day when I was made aware of some concern amongst our ratings. I had just returned to my cabin after breakfast when there was a knock on my door.

'Can I have a word with you, Second, please?' asked the donkeyman, the senior rating in our department. 'The Fourth Engineer has let me come up to see you for a few minutes,' he continued.

'OK, Donks, what's your problem?' I asked.

'Well, Sec, it looks as if there could be a strike in the not too distant future. I don't want to lose my job on this vessel. The rest of the lads feel the same. Is there anything that can be done to safeguard our jobs?' he asked.

'To be perfectly honest, Donks, I doubt it. But I'll make some enquiries at the London Pool when we return, and if there is anything I can do about the matter, you can rest assured I certainly will,' I replied.

'Can I pass that on to the others, Sec?'

'You certainly can, but remember, no promises, OK?'

He nodded in the affirmative and departed.

Once again, our stopover time in Norrkoping was relatively brief with no opportunity to go ashore and we were soon Stockholm bound.

It was an early evening arrival on my watch and, after a shower, I planned not to be too late turning in. I was penning a letter to my girlfriend in Kent when I detected female voices from the Chief's cabin next door. They certainly sounded too young to be any of our passengers. My curiosity was more than a little aroused, but I needed an excuse to intervene without giving the game away.

'Sorry to trouble you, Chief,' I said, knocking on his cabin door. 'I've used up all my airmail paper. Have you any spare you can let me have, please?'

'Come in, Sec. Don't stand on the threshold looking like a lost sheep. I'd like you to meet these two young ladies. I'll sort out your paper problems later.'

The Chief seemed genuinely pleased to welcome me in.

'First of all, please meet my next-door neighbour's daughter from back home. Jane. This young man, Jane, is our Second Engineer, and his name is Paul,' the Chief explained.

We exchanged the usual pleasantries.

'This young lady is Jane's Swedish penfriend of very long standing. Please meet Ulrika,' he continued.

I sensed a feeling almost of déjà vu. Ulrika bore a striking resemblance to the girl I had met briefly in Gothenburg on my last trip on the *Hydra*.

I was soon acquainted with their respective immediate life histories, with the Chief providing ample drinks to assist the storytellers. As the evening wore on, Ulrika had other things on her mind and, without further ado, invited herself to my cabin when her English friend decided it was time to depart. The Chief shrugged his shoulders and said he would get a taxi for her. Ulrika chatted briefly with her friend, bid her farewell then took me by my hand and led me into my cabin.

Now grasping both of my hands, Ulrika invited me to her home and suggested that I stay the night. Her parents, who owned one of the department stores in Stockholm, were away on holiday so no explanations would be necessary. There was absolutely no doubt what this lovely lass had in her mind. She didn't even want me to bother to change out of my uniform or waste time taking a shower. I felt totally torn. Here was a heaven sent opportunity on a plate, almost too good to be true. But how could I face my girlfriend in Kent again, if I gave in to this temptation?

'Ulrika, what can I say? I am extremely flattered to be asked to come to your home. I also find it extremely difficult to decide what to do. I am simply no good at deceiving people, least of all the opposite sex, and in particular my girlfriend back home. She certainly wouldn't understand if she found out that I had stayed the night at your home,' I pleaded.

'Paul, you Englishmen are unbelievable. Nobody is going to tell your girl in England. Let us walk along the quay towards the entrance gate,' she suggested.

We did just that. The further we walked and talked, the more guilty I felt.

'Look, Ulrika, I'll get you a taxi. Let's leave things as they are this trip and I'll hope to see you next time when I've had time to think things over, OK?'

Of course it wasn't. I had only succeeded in convincing one more Swedish girl that some Englishmen left a lot to be desired in at least one department. I also had a feeling I'd just made the biggest mistake of my life for what seemed, at that time, all the right reasons. One thing for certain, I would just have to hope and pray word did not get to my girlfriend when she next boarded. After all, having been seen leaving the ship late at night with a beautiful Swedish blonde would take some explaining away.

'How do you do manage to win 'em over then, Sec?' enquired my watch mate on passage to Gavle next day. 'I saw you disappearing into the distance last night with that blonde bombshell on your arm. Thought to myself, lucky mucky sod.'

'No, no. You saw nothing of the sort my good man. It was all a mirage, even in these climes, OK?' I threatened in a less than friendly manner.

I was looking forward to the Second Mate's safe arrival party at Gavle. The action all took place on board the vessel with little chance for any misunderstandings, misconceptions or even conceptions arising, but then I did not envisage the programme that would follow.

'We're having a film show tonight, Paul, instead of the usual entertainment,' the Second Mate promised, shortly after we berthed.

'You are joking, Dave? That doesn't compare with the normal party fare you offer,' I replied.

'I should wait and see. They haven't designated a rating yet in the UK for what probably will be on offer.'

It turned out that the PO's mess room had been commandeered for projection purposes, presumably because it was remote from the passenger accommodation. Once again, the Second Mate had been using his entrepreneurial skills to earn a little on the side. 'Blue' films were regularly shown in Continental cinemas but were still the exception rather than the rule in the UK. What was shown that evening could only be termed deep blue. Copies were available to purchase, if so required, but the penalty for being caught bringing such artwork into the country was not just steep but vertically inclined.

'Well, what did you think, Paul?' enquired the Second Mate next day.

'If you want an honest opinion, Dave, I'll settle for your poker parties any day,' I replied.

'Could be a problem there. According to the Old Man, the seamen's strike is almost a certainty. In fact it may even have started by the time we dock in London,' he added.

Once again, during the return voyage, the department ratings pleaded for promises to be given to secure their jobs on the vessel but, sadly, I could not give the assurances they and their Swedish girlfriends so desperately sought.

33

'Second, pop up topside for a few minutes, will you? I'm afraid the news is not good at all,' the Chief Engineer advised me on the engine room telephone, not long after we berthed in the Millwall Dock, London.

I'd guessed the Chief's news was directly related to the looming strike situation and I was not wrong. The Deck Department's Superintendent had met the vessel on arrival and informed the Captain that we would not be going anywhere in the near future because the strike had commenced and the officers' union had agreed with the National Union of Seamen not to intervene to hijack their actions.

'Where does this leave us then, Chief?' I asked.

'I'm still waiting for more instructions, but I understand we shall only be able to carry out basic operations in port, like keeping the fuel tanks topped up and checking safety matters. The shore gang that's coming on board will be responsible for dealing with everything else. I don't think the Port Authorities will relax their rules requiring some officers to remain on board at all times, however,' he added.

'I'm more than willing to stand by the vessel in London, Chief, as you can imagine,' I volunteered.

'Me likewise, Second, but we shall just have to see what the office want us to do,' he replied.

It was decided by the powers that be that our good vessel required to be manned by the Captain and one deck officer, the Chief Engineer and myself, but neither the Chief Steward or any members of the Catering Department would be on board. We would be required to look after our own accommodation but would not be allowed access to the galley or provision stores, therefore we could not feed ourselves on board. A basic meals allowance would be paid to enable us to buy our meals in local eating establishments.

The Chief suggested that I collect my car from my sister's home in Kent then return the following morning. He was not intending to use his own car in London because he could be home in about an hour and a half using the train, but my car would prove very useful for transporting the four of us to our chosen eating places. There were certainly no flies on the Chief and probably no contribution from him either for my petrol expenses.

I could only hope Christine would appreciate that whilst it looked as if my vessel was going to be tied up in London for some considerable time, I was not going to be able to escape to Kent at the drop of a hat.

'Paul, I can easily come up on the train to town at the weekend so there shouldn't be any problem,' she suggested when we discussed the matter that evening.

'There won't be food available on board, we'll be eating ashore at nearby cafés but that will be a change at least, I suppose. I'm not sure what your mum will make of it, though,' I replied.

We agreed to play things by ear, as it was too early to say what was going to happen in the next week or so.

My recollection of the next few weeks or so as the strike dragged on is a mixture of organized chaos and amazing revelations, with life leading one in totally unexpected directions.

Our relief Second Mate knew the East End of London and its pubs like the back of his hand. His only expertise in food-related matters however, was, unfortunately, Chinese takeaways. More by good luck than anything else, we did discover some excellent eating houses almost within striking distance of the vessel, which proved a blessing for breakfast and midday meals. This naturally suited the others down to the ground. The Second Mate couldn't wait to take off for more adventurous venues in the evening and, at his direction, we ate and drank in many different watering holes varying from a Thames-side pub in Richmond to London Airport.

'Tony, my girlfriend is coming up to London tomorrow. Why don't you join us for a night on the town?' I suggested one evening as we returned from yet another trip ashore.

He gratefully accepted my invitation, so I further suggested he choose the venue and keep it a secret. I had decided to take a leaf out of the Chief Engineer's book. If the night turned out to be a flop, I could hardly be blamed. Time would tell whether or not I had played with fire once too often.

I suppose the first hint that things could turn out to be somewhat different from usual that evening arose as we headed towards Victoria Station to meet my girlfriend. I was concentrating on my driving in heavy traffic and didn't at first appreciate the significance of the Second Mate's question.

'Paul, how much do you reckon the tickets cost for the three of us tonight?' he asked.

'You mean, how much do I owe you, Tony?'

'If you like then. What do you reckon?'

'Well, that depends on the venue. If it's a show or concert, I would guess around forty pounds. Almost a week's wages,' I offered in response.

'Not a bad guess at all, Paul. Just a few pounds more but very good value for money,' he added.

Of course, he knew I had a yearning for jazz. The one venue in London that was attracting an increasing following in this type of music was Ronnie Scott's club. But it was only as we drove from the station after collecting my girlfriend and were heading back into the West End that he revealed our destination.

'You're joking, of course,' I ventured.

157

'Now would I do that?' he replied.

There appeared to be no doubt at all in my girlfriend's mind that he wasn't kidding.

'Paul, I bet you can't guess who we are about to see live,' she excitingly exclaimed.

'No, I haven't a clue. Nor have you, I reckon.'

Then the penny dropped. Almost like a ton weight. It was becoming increasingly possible for one or two American artists to appear in the UK without upsetting Equity, mainly by confining their appearances to clubs like Ronnie Scott's in the heart of the West End. I just happened to know that one particular artist was really hankering to perform over here.

'If it's a pianist we are destined to see, I'll guess at Dave Brubeck. In other words, "Take Five" live.'

'Spot on, Paul,' chimed in Tony. 'How about that then?'

He certainly had come up trumps as far as I was concerned. I had not expected to see the great man performing at that point in time.

Memories of that night linger to this day. The atmosphere in the club was electric, the music even more so, with the clientele, including ourselves, mesmerised by the dexterity displayed before our very eyes with Paul Desmond on alto sax, Eugene Wright on bass and Joe Morello on drums.

Memories of the seamen's strike also linger but not always for the best of reasons. Obviously it was great to see my girlfriend on a regular basis, there was also much to be gained from seeking out and enjoying our eating haunts and even an evening out at London Airport had its moments. However, we were beginning to experience major problems in trying to keep our act together on board the vessel in such difficult times. Vital maintenance was getting over-looked and problems kept cropping up for the shore-based personnel who were trying their best in impossible circumstances.

'How much longer do you reckon this fiasco is going to

last, Tony?' I asked the Second Mate one day, on returning topsides after sorting out one more problem down below.

'Well, it looks as if the Seamen's Union are hearing what they want to from the powers that be, so I would imagine they'll call off the strike in the near future,' he surmised.

Then, once again, the unexpected happened.

The Chief Engineer had some news for me when he returned to the vessel after his weekend off.

'Second, I received a telephone call at home from our London Superintendent. He asked me to inform you that there is a rescheduling of personnel going on at the present time and that in all probability you will be sailing as Second Engineer on the *Lyra* from your home port to Norway, once the strike is over. I wouldn't imagine that news will go down well with your girlfriend,' he added.

'You're absolutely correct with that assumption, Chief. Just when I thought I was on to a good thing ... I can hardly believe the news. Did he say when he wanted me to return North?'

'No, he didn't mention that but I would imagine probably in about two weeks' time, the way things look as if they're going with the strike,' he replied.

I dreaded passing on the news to my girlfriend.

'It's just not fair, Paul. Why on earth can't they just leave you where you are?' she sobbed.

'I haven't a clue, my love. Unfortunately in this vocation, personal considerations don't figure very high in the planning strategy. At least I shall be home frequently, so I should be able to get down to see you whenever I'm relieved,' I volunteered.

I was not at all sure this would happen all that often. My past experience was that home port reliefs were only available infrequently; but I daren't tell her that.

34

I had barely enough time to sort myself out before it was time to join my new vessel. The seamen's strike was called off even sooner than had been expected, therefore subsequent events took place with unprecedented rapidity.

My journey home had been tinged with great regret. I was leaving behind so much that I wanted to hang onto quite desperately. Although I knew I was joining one of the most popular vessels in the fleet, with both crews and passengers, and the Norwegian ports of call were a delight in themselves, I just wished the vessel was sailing from London.

Once again, I had the welcome opportunity to sign on the best crew available as the ship's articles were opened almost immediately after the finish of the strike. I hadn't previously sailed with any of the engineers before but I remembered the Mate from a previous vessel. The Chief Engineer was notorious for his outspoken opinions, particularly if correctness or fairness was in question or under scrutiny. His Scottish ancestry, however, appeared to create all kind of difficulties for him in pursuing his chosen goals. Even he realised that his dogmatic approach to life was at odds with his most innermost feelings, to such an extent that he felt it necessary to occasionally moderate his ideas or, more frequently, drown his doubts in an alcoholic haze. Whilst in an inebriated state, his hostility towards those who dared to disagree with him transposed him into a real villain of the piece. He had spent a good deal of his sea service in the company down the Mediterranean and his notoriety had earned him the nickname of 'Mad Fred of the Med'. Although I had heard about his exploits in the past and relieved on vessels in port with him, this was the first time I had sailed with him.

'I've heard we're carrying circus animals to Oslo this trip. Is that right, Chief?' I enquired.

'Ay, laddie and they are parking one on deck right outside my ruddy cabin,' he replied. 'A bloody great elephant, the Mate tells me.'

'Really,' said I, and then promptly wondered who would kick up the most fuss.

'I take it that there's nothing for us to deal with concerning the animals, Chief?'

'Certainly not, laddie. Just keep out of the way of the ruddy things. The trainers will do the necessary. They'd better have large shovels and know how to use them, otherwise I shall have their guts for garters,' he thundered, visually turning slightly redder than normal.

The thought did cross my mind that in an emergency and without any contribution from the Chief, life could get a trifle difficult for those onboard, particularly with the animals concerned. But I decided not to press the point, or I could well see emergency muster lists of an unprecedented nature appearing.

It transpired that we were not carrying any of the large cats, just the elephants, horses and dogs. This should have been a great comfort to us, although the difference between having one's head bitten off or being trampled underfoot by a couple of tons of hoofed trunking, I could not begin to comprehend.

The elephant trainer turned out to be a relatively young man, very knowledgable, who did not anticipate having any problems with his charges unless the weather deteriorated. But then, apparently, air travel suited the elephants even less and as for rail transport, he would rather not recall his memories of the derailment that almost ended in disaster.

161

'Tell me, Dick,' I asked him during the crossing, 'what would happen if Rose here decided she would like to take a walk along the deck instead of being cooped up in that cage?'

'To be perfectly honest, there is just about nothing that one could do to prevent her. She's quite strong enough to break her ankle chains and could demolish this cage in about two minutes if she put her mind to it,' he replied.

'Thanks a million. I think I'd better warn the Chief just in case he feels the need to bawl at her when she starts trumpeting while he's asleep,' I suggested.

'I don't think we'll have any trouble with her, but as for one or two of the others, I'm not so sure,' he commented.

Surprisingly enough, even though the weather worsened before we reached Oslo Fjord, our animal passengers were generally less trouble than their human counterparts. At least with the animals, one was spared the usual jibes about the bad driving antics of the Deck Department every time the vessel rolled or pitched uncomfortably.

Rose's trainer was more concerned about what would happen after the vessel berthed.

'The only trouble I can foresee happening is when the time comes to lift her off. If she thinks she is going to be travelling next on a train, she'll more than likely try to break out of her cage. Don't ask me how she can sense what transport is awaiting her but she's never known to be wrong. We've even tried to fool her by bringing road transport down specially, but somehow she knows it's not for her.'

'Can't you sedate her then?' I enquired.

'No, I'm afraid not in this situation. She has to transfer herself between her deck cage and into a lifting container, then, once ashore, she transfers herself onto her next transport,' her trainer explained.

When it came to lifting Rose off the vessel, I watched, like the others, with a fair degree of apprehension. Whilst in mid-flight she obviously came to the conclusion that rail transport was awaiting her and certainly was having nothing to do with it. One could only describe the crane driver as either a genius, a gambler or a hero, but somehow, one way or another, before his crane toppled over and before the bottom dropped out of the container, Rose was landed safely in one piece on the quay. I could only marvel at the patience and dedication of her trainer and the rest of the circus staff who eventually coaxed Rose into continuing her journey by road.

'She's not the best of travellers, but by hell she makes up for it in the ring.' The trainers words lingered in my thoughts as they disappeared out of view.

I didn't plan on paying a visit to the Big Top. There were far more intriguing venues to be sought out. I just hoped that at some time whilst serving on the *Lyra* the opportunity would arise to explore a few of the unique sights worth seeing in Oslo.

My scrutiny of the pamphlets on board the vessel suggested that the Kon-Tiki Museum housing Thor Heyerdahl's balsawood raft on which he and five companions drifted 5,000 miles across the Pacific Ocean in 1947 might just be one of many locations not to be missed. Again, the Viking Ships Exhibition looked promising, with three of these vessels on display. One more destination which I already knew about was the Vigeland Sculpture Park with its unusual displays of human forms interacting with one another in very interesting ways. One building was impossible to miss. That was the Town Hall. This mammoth building, visible from the vessel's berth, was built between 1931 and 1950 and completed just in time to mark the ninth centenary of the founding of Oslo.

My thoughts were abruptly interrupted by the Chief Engineer.

'Second, can we have a few words? I don't intend to interfere with your running of the department but I need to know how you propose to schedule the routine maintenance work. We don't have any repairs carried out back in the UK, you know, only boiler cleaning,' he added.

'Well, Chief, nothing different to usual. I'll be looking

after the main engine cylinders, valve and running gear and the Third Engineer will be dealing with the remainder. The Fourth will look after the pumps and auxiliaries. Provided no unusual problems crop up, I can't imagine that we shall have any problems, time-wise,' I replied.

'What about your stores requisitioning, laddie? We don't need to overstock for these shortish voyages. You'll end up having surplus items crossed off your list if you overdo it, you know,' he continued.

'That won't be a problem, Chief. I've no intention of over-ordering. I'm only interested in maintaining an adequate level of stores and spare gear, rest assured.'

35

Whilst I was quite pleased about sailing on my new vessel, thoughts of my girlfriend and the South of England were never far from my mind. I just cursed my misfortune that the seamen's strike had intervened when it did. Losing the *Aries* in this manner, and my direct contact with the south, really only struck me later on.

Our Chief Engineer was not the most understanding individual when it came to personal matters. As far as he was concerned, the department came first in all respects and woe betide anybody or anything that intervened to upset this. Such an event occurred on our return to the UK. The Fourth Engineer's wife arrived by taxi with their young family shortly after we berthed.

'Second, will you just remind the Fourth Engineer that I require the fuel in the number four double bottom fuel tanks transferring before he departs, just in case he thinks he can shoot off now,' the Chief demanded.

'Surely the fuel can be transferred tomorrow, Chief? We've no urgent requirements for it.'

'Second, I do not want the tank heating left on any longer. It is a wasteful exercise. So just do as I ask, would you,' he growled, getting redder in the face by the second.

'OK, Chief, whatever you say. Leave it with me,' I replied.

I knocked on the Fourth Engineer's cabin door and passed on the glad tidings.

'No problem, Sec, I'm well used to his demands. That's why I haven't changed yet. A couple of trips back, he waited until I'd showered and changed then suddenly remembered he required a pump opening up for survey the following morning. That little exercise was intended to save the company a couple of hours' shore labour expense,' he replied.

'As far as I am concerned, Fourth, that won't be happening while I am Second Engineer. The Chief can make sure he lets me know what his requirements are in good time, otherwise he'll be a disappointed man, I can assure you.'

I telephoned my girlfriend as soon as I could. Her first question made me bitterly regret that I hadn't made a few enquires beforehand.

'When will you be travelling down to see me, Paul?' she asked eagerly.

'Well, Christine, I'm not sure whether I shall be able to get away, this time back. We haven't been advised whether there will be any reliefs for us yet. We should know by tomorrow,' I replied.

'Can't you ask for a few days' leave instead of waiting for a relief?' she countered.

'I wish it was as easy as that, my love. These days, you have to give about a month's notice to be able to take leave, even when you're not asking to leave a vessel.'

Of course, I was on a hiding to nothing unless a miracle happened the following day. Even my parents detected that I was caught in a cross-fore situation.

'You have only yourself to blame, Paul,' my dear mother decided. 'You should not have led Christine to believe that you would be traipsing off south to suit her beck and call.'

I had no intention of getting involved in an argument with my mother, so I didn't pursue the matter any further.

Back on board the vessel the following morning, the news was not unexpected. There would be no reliefs for us this voyage but every attempt would be made to provide reliefs at the end of the next one. Knowing the unpredictability of the relief forecasting, none of us were filled with optimism but at least I did have some news to pass on to my girlfriend next time we spoke to one another.

One distinct advantage of standing by the vessel in port

as Second Engineer was the opportunity to personally supervise all that was being done by the shore personnel in the engine room. Their main involvement was cleaning the boilers and testing them afterwards. It almost goes without saying that when you are sailing on a vessel, you take a very personal interest in making sure the job is done properly and that all is well afterwards, otherwise the resulting problems cause a little more than simply heartache.

'Don, there are still several leakages from the superheater element joints. Can you get your lads to have another go, please,' I requested the shore side foreman.

'I don't think you have a problem, Sec. Those joints will take up once the boiler pressure increases,' he insisted.

'I've heard that one before. In my experience, they rarely do. So, if you could at the very least follow up the headers, then we can carry out a retest,' I insisted.

The shore repeairers did not have to face the consequences of their occasional lapses, which in some respects was a great pity.

One further advantage of standing by as Second Engineer was the knowledge that, come hell or high water, one's departure from the vessel each day at a reasonable time was almost certainly guaranteed. The superintendents were always certain to make their ship visits during the latter part of the morning, apart from in exceptional circumstances. This allowed the Chief Engineer to depart in good time, knowing full well that shortly afterwards the Second Engineer would do likewise, leaving matters in the capable hands of the two junior ranking engineers.

I only wished that my love life could be as well ordered as my working life. My attempts to pour oil on troubled waters as far as my girlfriend was concerned were not all that successful. Her mother, once again, was not convinced that my efforts to keep in touch were all that commendable.

'Paul, you can hardly expect my daughter to be delighted by your unpredictability. Let's face it, whenever she needs you, you are not around. That is surely not the way to encourage her fondness for you, now is it?' she questioned.

'I only wish there was some way that things could be changed, but you know as well as I do that I can't demand leave at a moment's notice. The company only grant leave at short notice for family bereavement or serious illness,' I replied.

I would possibly have achieved more if I had simply just agreed with her. In many respects, I couldn't wait to be back to sea again.

The day before we sailed, the Stewardess had a bit of interesting news for me.

'Paul, our passenger list suggests a real mixed bunch of characters, of both sexes. Could be quite an interesting voyage, I think. I'll keep you posted when I know more,' she added.

'As long as there are no MPs, barristers, sky pilots, female bank directors and doctors and/or their daughters, I'll be happy.' I knew just how complicated life can get on board when such types expound their points of view to one and all, particularly after imbibing their particular favourite liquid refreshment. I also had in mind recollections of the misunderstandings that my colleagues had come across in the past. Sometimes the effort required to sort out other people's intoxicated misdemeanours was beyond all reasonable expectation.

As we proceeded downriver after clearing the docks, I was taking a refreshing breather on deck and being updated by our Stewardess with regard to the passengers.

'Well, as I told you, Paul, they are a right mixture. We have a professional photographer and his wife, a vicar with his wife, a lady school teacher and her friend, a couple of climbers and a party of holiday tour representatives,' she reported.

'I think I shall be keeping a low profile by choice, Jean,' I replied.

As she returned to the accommodation, I pondered to what extent, if any, our passengers' diverse backgrounds would influence the atmosphere on board.

36

As sea crossings go in autumn, we had a relatively smooth trip with no particular problems. Both the Third and Fourth Engineers were competent and reliable, the Third Engineer having himself sailed as Second Engineer under a dispensation from the BOT.

Our progress up the Oslo Fjord that evening was to be a sight for sore eyes. Having just come off watch at 8.00 pm., I stole the opportunity to take a passenger-eye view of the vista ahead. We were still some way from Oslo but the city lights were just discernible on the distant horizon. My heart missed a beat as a high-speed hydrofoil passenger craft flew past us, almost shaving the side of our vessel. This craft was also heading towards Oslo and, judging from its progress, it would be passing us again in a short while, heading in the opposite direction on a return trip.

The amount of water-borne traffic in the fjord should not have been surprising but when this varies from translantic passenger liners to two-berth cabin cruisers all sharing the same waterway, one can only marvel at the skill and professionalism of those navigating the larger vessels along the fjord.

After we had berthed, I decided to take a brief rest before showering and changing.

The Chief Engineer peered round the door of my cabin. 'Second, what do you reckon? Do I look all right? It's my neet tonight, och ay.'

I looked once, then again.

'And what are ye staring at, laddie?' he growled. The familiar reddening was permeating through his jowls.

'Well, Chief, just one or two little things, minor in themselves, I suppose. First of all, you're wearing a uniform jacket with sports trousers. Then there's your brightly coloured shirt, no tie. Surely that can't be right. And what the hell have you got on your hair?' I asked.

The trouble was that having a good head of steam and firing on all cylinders in that condition his unpredictability was legendary. Nevertheless, on this occasion he appeared to genuinely require some assistance to guide him in the right direction.

He disappeared for a short while then reappeared.

'That's better Chief. Hey, wait a minute. What have you put on your hair now, for heaven's sake? I don't believe it, that's bloody shaving cream. It's going to have to come off.' I really had had enough.

'Stop bloody fussing, Sec. I'm losing time. Someone will have shanghaied her.' he groaned.

'And who might she be?' I asked.

'Never you bloody well mind. I've had my eye on her ever since we sailed.'

He wasn't prepared to stifle his enthusiasm a moment longer. Before anybody could intervene, he headed off in the general direction of the passenger lounge.

I sat and puzzled about who the unlucky lady could be. I decided it could only be a woman probably in her forties, apparently on her own and almost certainly a school teacher, possibly specialising in religious education with totally inflexible opinions. I had never thought of the Chief as a ladies' man before, although he did have a habit of frequently recalling his conquests of yesteryear with monotonous regularity.

A good hour later, whilst I was having a chat with the Second Mate in his cabin, sounds of discord percolated down from the upper deck.

'I just hope to hell that is not the Chief performing. I know only too well he's capable of wreaking mayhem for all concerned,' I said.

170

The sounds got louder by the minute, the voices harder by the second. Then the unmistakeable tones of the Captain drowned out all other conversation.

'Chief, this way, if you please. I'll speak to you in your cabin but first you will apologise to this lady,' he demanded.

'That doesn't sound too good,' I suggested. 'I'm keeping out of the way until morning. We'll have to try to sort things out when the Chief has sobered up, I reckon.'

'He's an absolute pain in the arse, if you ask me. How the hell he gets away with it, I'm blessed if I know,' the Second Mate considered.

'He's not too bad when sober, Dick, but once he's had a skinful, he's bloody impossible,' I added.

Next morning, before breakfast, there was a familiar knock on my cabin door.

'Morning, Chief. Come on in if you want,' I said, as I glanced at his face. One look said it all.

'I've put my bloody big foot in it this time, Second, I'm afraid. It's bound to be the high jump for me, I reckon,' he groaned.

'Really, Chief?' I tried to sound dumbfounded. 'How on earth could such a thing happen to a gentleman like you?'

'Och aye, laddie, something I said, I reckon,' the Chief volunteered.

'Like what?' I enquired.

'Och, I dunno, something about being a frigid bitch, I think, but I didna say it to her face.'

'Eh! What!' I exclaimed.

'Well, you know, laddie, how it is. I'd had a few and just fancied her . . .'

'Say no more, Chief. There's still a long way to go before the end of the trip. I'll try to repair some of the damage if I can, but please, please, keep clear of her, otherwise you'll be heading back down the Med or even worse,' I threatened.

For the next few days, he lived in virtual isolation from everyone except those in his department. I plucked up courage to speak to the lady in question when she appeared on the boat deck whilst I was checking the lifeboat.

'Could I have a word with you, if you don't mind?' I asked. 'As you've probably gathered, I am the Second Engineer and my name is Paul James. I've heard about the Chief's unforgivable rudeness directed at you in the passenger lounge the other day. I just want to apologise on behalf of all of us and hope that it hasn't spoilt your holiday.'

'That is very kind of you, Second. No, it hasn't spoilt my holiday. I do understand, you know,' she replied, calmly and quietly.

'I beg your pardon,' I said, 'Did I hear you right?'

She smiled, almost shyly. 'Yes, you did. You probably aren't going to believe what I am about to tell you. You see, my father was a chief engineer. He had a drink problem, just like your Chief. Obviously he shouldn't have said what he did, especially in front of the other passengers. It was extremely embarrassing, particularly for Reverend Amby. He tried to intervene and was less than politely told by your Chief to mind his own so-and-so business.'

'Well, all I can say is that I think you are a very charming and understanding lady and the Chief is extremely lucky it was you he chose to be so rude to,' I commented.

'Paul,' she said, 'I am not sure the Chief will think he is lucky when the ship gets back. The Reverend Amby has told me that he is making an official complaint to the company about the incident, despite my asking him to overlook the matter.'

'Oh dear. I'd better not mention that, but I will put the record straight with him about yourself, and thanks again for being so understanding,' I concluded.

Time would tell what the outcome for the Chief would be but, being aware of his reputation for survivability, I reckoned there was a fair chance he would be back again for the next trip.

37

Any thoughts that I might have had of doing a spot of sightseeing on this voyage evaporated into thin air when the Third Engineer succumbed to an accidental strain of his back during maintenance work in the engine room. I took over his night on board duties, also his electrical maintenance work throughout the vessel, which, coupled with my normal duties, left precious little time for anything else.

The Chief was extremely subdued, almost apologetic at times, so much so that I felt almost obliged to offer him some reassurance.

'There's no point in fearing the worst, Chief,' I tried. 'The vicar will probably have a change of heart before we return to the UK. I know she was going to try and persuade him to drop the matter.'

'Ay, laddie, but what if he doesn't?' he lamented.

'Well, that could be a trifle difficult, I must admit. Surely an apology all round would do the trick,' I suggested.

'That depends on how many apologies they're prepared to take, Sec. Mind you, I haven't sent a written one in before,' he admitted.

'For heaven's sake, Chief, how many apologies have you previously made?' I enquired, almost in disbelief.

'Depends on how far you want to go back, Sec,' he replied, looking somewhat sheepish.

'How about over the last ten years then, Chief?' I tried.

'Och, not all that many, if I remember correctly. Could have been about, well, er, say four, probably five. I don't know. I don't keep a ruddy score sheet, you know,' he explained, not looking in my direction.

'Let's hope that common sense prevails, Chief. If I get an opportunity to have a little word in the cherubic ear of the vicar, who knows, I might get through to him.' I felt more like saying that if I did, I would also probably end up getting the old heave-ho as well, but I resisted the temptation to heap more agony on the Chief's troubled shoulders.

Fortunately he refrained from imbibing his favourite tipple for the remainder of the voyage, but a sober, unhappy Scot can be an even bigger cross to bear in close proximity than one who has gone well over the top, drink-wise. He obviously decided that in order to demonstrate that he was not a lost cause, there would be a need to show his superiors new-found responsibility, a new approach, something he could be proud of as Chief Engineer ... I was to be his chosen recipient to hear of his grand plan.

'Second, I wonder if you can spare a few minutes? I've got a wee bee in my bonnet, so to speak,' he asked, as I returned to my cabin following dinner next day.

'Sounds too good to miss, Chief,' I replied, trying to keep a straight face and voice.

'Don't be bloody cheeky, laddie. I'm being serious. It's going to be my new image,' he claimed. 'I want to be known as a forward-looking, money-saving, cost-effective Chief. How about that, Sec?' he swaggered.

'That sounds absolutely fine to me. But tell me please, just how are you going to achieve this new-found status?'

'Planned maintenance, laddie, that's what I'm going to call it,' he proudly announced.

'Really, Chief? You mean, working out in advance what needs to be done and then sticking to it?'

'That, Second, is a gross oversimplification. It's not as easy as that. First of all, you've got to work out what work needs to be done and how frequently. That procedure would apply to all the plant and machinery on board, but obviously priority work would have to come first, especially to prevent breakdowns,' he added.

174

I could see the discussion progressing ad infinitum, therefore taking the easiest way out seemed to be the simplest option.

'Well, Chief, I wish you well and hope the company appreciates your efforts and is well impressed,' I told him.

I listened enviously to the holiday tour representatives enthusiastically recounting their visits ashore, hoping that in the not too distant future I might also make a few interesting discoveries.

As the voyage progressed, I was tempted to raise the subject of the Chief with the lady in question, if only to find out whether or not she had succeeded in persuading the vicar to change his mind about reporting the Chief's indiscretion to the company on the vessel's return to the UK. Whilst I had little sympathy for the Chief in his predicament, nevertheless the prospect of his losing his vessel or even his job seemed poor reward for his undoubted diligence as an engineer.

Thoughts also dwelt in my mind about my desperate need to be relieved on arrival back, otherwise my prospects of continuing my friendship with Christine would be fast receding. Of one thing I was certain: provided I was relieved, my arrival in Kent would go unannounced until I appeared on my girlfriend's doorstep.

At least our passengers were apparently enjoying themselves, according to the Stewardess, with their enjoyment further increased by visiting the port of Drammen in the Drammen Fjord, just around the corner from the Oslo Fjord. Drammen is Norway's fifth biggest town, straddling the Drammen river. The panoramic views of the surrounding countryside and forested hills provide a never to be forgotten sight, with the Spiralen tunnel road taking one in six loops up to the top of the Bragernesasen mountain. Apparently, in the older parts of the town, there are still a large number of quaint old timber buildings from the days of the timber trade.

I let the Fourth Engineer go exploring during the afternoon, remembering my own ventures ashore under similar circumstances.

Fortunately, the Third Engineer made a dramatic recovery from his back problems and by next day we were on course, heading back home.

38

I was never sure quite what to expect in the way of a greeting from my girlfriend in Kent. This was the thought lingering in my mind as I sped southwards in my Sunbeam Alpine. I couldn't help but reflect on what my mother had said previously about the lack of continuity in my relationships and the problems that arose because of this. I was prepared, so I thought, for almost any eventuality. Probably a make or break situation would come about, mabye her mother would even give me my marching orders. Then again, my unannounced appearance on the scene might tell me more than I could ever want to hear. The one thing, however, that I hadn't dreamed of hearing was the news that really stopped me in my tracks as she greeted me in the garden of her home.

'Darling Paul, goodness knows what you're going to say when I tell you I think that I'm pregnant.'

I couldn't think straight, my brain was trying to calculate the important and relevant dates. I was lost for words.

'Are you all right, Paul? I hope you're not too upset?' she asked almost mournfully.

'Heavens, no, my love. But I can hardly take it in. Have you had a medical opinion yet?'

'No, but I'm pretty certain. Haven't told my mum yet. Goodness knows what she will say. I hardly dare think.'

Thoughts raced through my mind. It was time for action. One way or another I would find out just where I stood in Christine's line-up. After all, she hadn't said, in so many words, that I was the culprit.

'I think it's my turn to spring a surprise, Christine. If I said I would like to marry you, what would you say to that?' I uttered words that seemed to emanate from another planet and not my mouth.

I had obviously, thankfully, said the right things this time.

'Here's hoping the neighbours are not Peeping Toms, otherwise we'll have given them something to crow about,' I eventually gasped as I emerged from a death-defying embrace. 'Surely your answer can only be yes,' I added.

She looked me straight in the eyes, slowly nodding in the affirmative, her head slightly bowed but with a smile spreading all over her face.

'I think it would be best to tell your mother right away about our big news but nothing else at present. What do you reckon?' I asked.

'Whatever you say, Paul. When can I choose my ring, please, my love?' she hummed.

'We can pop over to Canterbury tomorrow, if you like, and see what's on offer,' I suggested.

Quite what my family would make of the news, I couldn't begin to imagine. After all, I had not even hinted about such a possibility before I departed for the south.

My sister Jennifer, her husband and daughter, however, were delighted, obviously thinking that we might decide to live in the south after our marriage, thereby ensuring a closer contact between us all.

Thankfully, Christine's mother raised no objection to our marriage plans but left me in no doubt whatsoever about what she thought would be the most suitable time to go ahead.

'After all, Paul, you can hardly expect Christine to sit at home wondering what you are up to in far away places. When do you hope to return to shore employment?'

'As soon as I have completed my seagoing certificates. In fact, I have already been invited to make career enquiries with one of the Classification Societies as a surveyor but they will only consider employing me if I hold all the relevant certificates before I apply,' I replied.

'I see, and how long, may I ask, will it take you to obtain these certificates?' she enquired.

'Hopefully, only about two or three more years at the most.'

'Well, at least you'll have a nice long engagement before taking the plunge,' she finally added.

I wondered how long she would expect us to wait if she knew that her daughter was pregnant but time would no doubt tell. When I mentioned this to Christine the following day during our trip to Canterbury, her response came as no surprise.

'Paul, my mum would expect you to abandon your sea-going career as soon as possible, I'm sure,' she replied.

Mixed emotions and doubts filled my thoughts as she spoke but I was certainly not going to either change my mind or give in to selfish pressures because of her mother's attitudes.

'Let's see if we can discover a ring to match your personality, Christine,' I suggested.

After what seemed an eternity, we found the ring. Just what she wanted and a delight to behold. Her mother, somewhat unexpectedly, had seemed not the least bit surprised by our engagement, I was even given a kiss on my cheek. No advice or recriminations were forthcoming either but I couldn't help but feel a twinge of guilt about keeping her in the dark about our other important news.

My visit to Kent swept by at an alarming speed, my thoughts frequently focussed on my fiancée's state but there was still one more surprise awaiting me before I departed. It came on the final evening as Christine and I tried to pretend that time had stood still. We hugged each other like there was no tomorrow, reluctant to part despite my departure time having well and truly passed.

'Hell, Christine, you know I don't want to leave you but there's a ship waiting for me to join in the morning and it's still three hundred and eighty odd miles away.'

'I know, Paul. I just don't want to say goodbye. Anyway,

you'll no doubt be relieved to hear that I'm not pregnant after all. It was a false alarm,' she whispered in my ear.

'Really? You're not joking, I hope.' She wasn't. 'Thank God for that, not literally, that is,' I added. It felt as if a ton weight had been taken off my shoulders.

It was only later that I would reflect on these events in more detail, but having finally managed to drag myself and my car away, my immediate concern was to try to make up for lost journey time, otherwise I would be getting no sleep at all before I rejoined my vessel next day.

It was November, and as I climbed up to the Thanet Way getting on for ten o'clock that evening, it didn't seem too bad a night for travelling, weatherwise. I had expectations of arriving back home by about 5 a.m. with three hours's sleep before reporting for duty. Could be worse, I thought.

But no sooner had I joined the Thanet Way than the visibility started to reduce with alarming rapidity. Within a mile, it was down to 100 yards. I just couldn't believe my misfortune. Then I suddenly remembered the special fog lights that had been fitted to the car. I had never needed to use them previously and reached for the switch to operate them, praying for good fortune. Again, my luck was not in. They would have lit up the heavens like a pair of search-lights if the dense fog had permitted. There was nothing else left for me to do but to creep along until I reached the motorway service station then try and adjust them there. It seemed an eternity until the slipway approach road eventu-ally appeared out of the murk, and gratefully I proceeded to the parking area and stopped the engine. Whether or not I had the right tools to do the job remained to be seen. As I peered into the car boot, a voice drifted towards me in the fog.

'Having trouble, sir?'

I looked up and glanced at the genuinely concerned face of a traffic policeman.

'Well, yes, I think you could say that. I've got a couple of fog lights that are about as useful to me as a basket full of newborn pups. How on earth skilled car mechanics could have done such a poor job of fitting them completely beats me,' I groaned.

'Right, young man. If you drive your car round to the other side of the parking area, you'll see a wall. Position the car facing the wall about twenty feet distant and I'll set them up for you in the same way that our patrol car lights are,' he kindly offered.

I gratefully accepted the officer's offer of assistance and, together with his colleague, he carefully measured the distances, marked the wall with chalk then set the lights to suit and secured them.

'How about that, then?' the officer suggested.

'Absolutely marvellous,' I exclaimed. 'Thank you very much indeed.'

'Where are you heading for?' he enquired.

'Yorkshire, and as soon as possible. I've a ship to join in the morning,' I replied.

'Well, you're going to have a demanding journey. The fog is stretching up to the Scottish Borders. Take care, watch your speed and have a safe journey,' he advised.

'Many thanks again,' I said as I headed off toward the slip road leading down to the motorway. I'd travelled barely 50 yards when a cacophony of sound blasted my ears and I squealed to a stop. Within seconds, the police car was alongside me.

'What's the matter?' I asked.

'You're heading towards the oncoming traffic if you go down that slipway,' they shouted in unison.

'Hell, sorry about that. I've got totally confused in the fog,' I pleaded quite reasonably I felt, in the circumstances.

They bid me farewell once again as I turned round and headed in the opposite direction towards the correct slip road.

Once on the motorway, my correctly adjusted lights provided positive illumination of both the nearside and centre lane catseyes and all I had to do was concentrate as hard as I could on the road immediately ahead, sitting on the edge of my seat with my nose almost pressed onto the windscreen. I had done the journey on so many previous occasions and had been known to proclaim that I knew the route so well I could cover the distance with my eyes closed. Well, it looked as if the moment of truth had arrived.

London turned out to be not too much of a problem, and as I headed out into the open country on the A1, I counted my lucky stars that I had been fortunate enough to have had the help of two knowledgable and experienced traffic officers to correctly adjust my fog lights.

After a while and after passing laybys full of stationary traffic with little traffic under way, I had a feeling that I wasn't travelling alone. I glanced briefly in my rear view mirror then stared again. Unless I was mistaken, I was at the head of a long, slow-moving convoy. As I exited the next roundabout, a quick backwards glance confirmed that the traffic following me stretched apparently endlessly. I couldn't help but feel sorry about abandoning my convoy role but it wouldn't be long before I turned off the A1.

It was certainly proving to be the most demanding road journey I had ever undertaken and after arriving safely home, before falling off to sleep on the settee I vowed to myself that I would never again attempt such a journey in November for any reason whatsoever.

39

'You look absolutely shattered, Paul. What on earth have you been up to?'

I had bumped into the Stewardess shortly after boarding the vessel, only just before sailing time and much to the displeasure of the Chief Engineer.

'Well, Joan, I've just got engaged, but it's nothing to do with that really. You could say that I'm a little short on sleep. I spent all last night driving back up north through dense fog and only managed a couple of hours' shut-eye, I'm afraid,' I replied.

'Well then, you had better keep out of the way of our illustrious passenger, at least until you've recovered. Otherwise he might write all the wrong things about you,' she quipped.

'You're kidding, of course?'

'No, not at all. He's the travel writer for the *Sunday Express*. And he's on business, to write about us lot, so he says.'

'Cor blimey, Joan, I think I'll hibernate. I don't fancy an inquisition,' I almost hesitated to say.

As it turned out, he was a true gentleman: courteous, and seemingly quite content to relax and enjoy the duty-free drinks and cigarettes whilst he had the opportunity to do so. He certainly seemed well enough pleased with the service he was getting on board the vessel, but quite what he would make of the Engineering Department, only time would tell.

I wasn't at all sure of whether the Chief Engineer was

aware of the potential threat to us all if he inadvertently crossed swords with the guy. After all, no journalist, whatever his persuasion, is going to throw away a good story just out of sympathy for his victims. I decided that we might live to regret it if I didn't forewarn the Chief.

I'd just come off watch and on leaving the engine room, I knocked on the Chief's cabin door.

'It's only me, Chief. I've brought the log book in case you want it. The Stewardess tells me we've got a gent from the press on board as a passenger. Apparently he writes on travel for the *Sunday Express*,' I advised.

'You don't say, Sec. Well, we've got nothing to hide. Och laddie, you show him round the engine room. That'll give him something to write about,' the Chief replied, totally missing the point and, in particular, the thoughts that were passing through my mind.

I was still bemused by how he had missed getting the chop after the fracas of the previous voyage. Despite this, he obviously saw no potential threat whatsoever to his own position or that of the department. I just prayed and hoped that we had no female passengers on board that would tempt him to risk his neck once again.

I decided to risk breakfast in the saloon next day. I did not expect our intrepid journalist to surface on his first morning; probably he would elect to have breakfast in his cabin. But no sooner had I seated myself at the Captain's table than he showed up looking exceptionally bright and breezy.

We exchanged the usual pleasantries and I assured him that those on duty down below were turning the paddles fast and furious in order to keep up our schedule. I then hastily reassured him I was only kidding and that should he wish to confirm matters concerning the method of propulsion used, he was more than welcome to take a look for himself.

'No thanks, Second. It's very kind of you to invite me down below but that's not quite my cup of tea, so to speak.

I prefer to leave such matters to those who know what they're doing,' he replied.

His main concern was to try and work out how much time he would have ashore at each of our stopping-off ports and which places they were likely to be. The Captain explained that, with a bit of luck, he would probably have plenty of time ashore in about five of the twelve or so ports we were due to visit around the fjords and coast of southern Norway. What the gentleman could not have been aware of, after we berthed in Oslo, was that the city centre was only a few minutes' walking distance from the vessel.

How well acquainted he was with the city he didn't reveal to us, but he was full of praise for the tours and sightseeing spots. He was quite amazed by the vista of the islands, with the distant sun penetrating the trees, leaving stark shadows streaking across the silky smooth surface of the fjords and mountain-sides. Truly a visual delight, even for those of us well used to such sights. The nightlife also seemed to appeal to him, and after exploring the usual vistor attractions including the Viking Ship exhibitions, he even found the shopping to his liking. Quite honestly, I was beginning to form the conclusion that short of falling overboard, there was little he would not find to his satisfaction, surely an unusual situation for a travel writer to find himself in, but probably not for this particular person. Nevertheless, we were beginning to wonder whether or not he was trying things on a bit for our benefit, giving us a false sense of security, only to disclose a totally different story to his readers. Time, as always, would tell.

The Chief displayed his usual amount of indiscretion in the circumstances.

'Och, laddie, I wouldn't trust that bugger further than I could throw him,' he growled in his predictable manner that evening, after listening to the gentleman enthusing about his day's adventures over dinner.

'He seems genuine enough to me, Chief, but I must acknowledge his criticisms are few and far between. Not what you would normally expect from a travel writer, I have to admit,' I replied. 'I can't wait to see what he has to say in the *Sunday Express*, like everyone else, no doubt.'

Once again, my Christmas shopping had almost got overlooked. I did manage to procure a selection of Norwegian traditional gifts in haste. After all, there was every possibility we would be back in the UK just before Christmas, provided we maintained out sailing schedule. I just prayed and hoped that I would be able to travel south to see my fiancée over Christmas, otherwise I was likely to end up in the doghouse. Her mum would certainly not tolerate any excuses that I might come up with, if the worst came to the worst, and Christine would be extremely disappointed. However, dwelling on the subject would not improve my well-being, therefore I decided to put the matter to the back of my mind and just hope for the best.

I did feel tempted to introduce our friend from the press to the realities of a seafarer's way of life but resisted, for the sake of peace of mind.

We were managing to stay on schedule and things were looking very promising. I remained optimistic until the Chief let go a bombshell shortly after departing from the Norwegian coast.

'Second, come down to my cabin after breakfast. The Old Man has had a message from the office. It's about the Christmas relief arrangements when we get back. I'll explain it to you,' he added.

A feeling of trepidation crept through me. I feared the worse.

'Come on in, Second,' the Chief called out a short while later, as I passed by his cabin.

'No reliefs, then, Chief, I suppose?' I enquired. 'Just like when I was sailing out of London.'

'What the Old Man says is that the office have advised him there are going to be more than the usual number of ships in port over the Christmas period, therefore the relief mates and engineers are going to be thinly spread around. This means that those who have recently had time off will have to stand by over Christmas to enable the others to share the available reliefs.'

'I ought to get that in writing, Chief, because my fiancée and her mother just won't believe it if I tell them that.'

'Ay, laddie, I wouldn't doubt that. Maybe something can be sorted out when we get back, so don't give up hope,' he replied.

40

It didn't take very long for my mother to detect the disappointment I was feeling about the relief situation over the Christmas holiday period. I had only arrived home from the ship that afternoon when she suggested that, at least, I should count myself lucky to have got back in time for Christmas.

'Surely, Paul, if you explain the situation to Christine, she will realise it's not your fault if you aren't able to travel down,' my mother suggested.

'I doubt it, Mum, and her mother certainly won't, I'm afraid,' I replied.

'Well, you are going to have to ring her up and say something, otherwise they will be extremely upset, you know. I know it's not fair, but you mustn't keep people in the dark,' she added.

Whether or not it was the sheer dread of making the wretched phone call or a feeling that the Chief knew something that I didn't but I decided to defer making the call until the following evening. By then, the situation on board the vessel would be much clearer. None of the other crew members were particularly bothered about the lack of reliefs. They all lived in the area and it was not going to be a problem to provide sufficient cover for each other.

The matter was very much on my mind when I boarded the vessel next morning. I couldn't see any way through the problem because not a single relief had turned up.

I was checking the store items in the engine room stores when I received a call from the Chief Engineer.

'Second, come up to my cabin, will you, right away. I've been asked to call in the office. I'm not sure what the Superintendent wants to see me about but there's another matter I might raise with him after I've spoken to you.'

I was still trying to work out what the Chief meant when I knocked on his cabin door.

'Right, Second, I've been giving this relief situation some thought. Being a Scotchman, celebrating Christmas doesn't fill me with good cheer. Provided I get my New Year break, I'll be happy to cover for you for Christmas Day and Boxing Day. What do you reckon?' he asked.

'Well, I hardly know what to say. You've left me almost speechless. You don't reckon the office will put the stoppers on it, then, if I accept?' I enquired.

'No, laddie. No problem at all, provided they know what's going on. I take it you'll be on your way tonight. Drive carefully and don't be late back or I'll have your guts for garters,' he threatened.

I thanked my lucky stars that I'd managed to buy a selection of Christmas presents in Oslo. Whether or not I would have time to get them wrapped up, would remain to be seen. My parents obviously had mixed feelings about my sudden unexpected departure for the south but I thanked my lucky stars one more time for deciding not to make that fateful telephone call the previous evening. I decided to contact my sister during the journey to let her know when I might arrive and leave it to her to pass on the news to my fiancée. Just when you want time to stand still for a while, the clock seems to spin out of control.

After what seemed an eternity gathering together all the items for my trip and getting them loaded, I eventually waved goodbye to my family and sped off. At least the weather was favourable for the time of the year and I reckoned that I would be passing through London about midnight, all things being equal. My telephone call could not wait that long.

'Hi there, Jennifer. Yes, it's Paul. Where am I? About eighty miles from London, heading south in your direction.

Would you be kind enough to let Christine know I'm on my way, please?' I asked.

My dear sister almost took it for granted that I was quite capable of springing out of the woodwork, so to speak and she would almost certainly have a meal ready on my arrival.

It would have been a lot better to have arrived earlier in the day but the welcome that I received, especially from my niece, made the journey very worthwhile.

'Paul, I'm not quite sure how to tell you this. I rang Christine's house to pass on your message and her mother was quite abrupt with me. Apparently Christine has gone away for a few days to see friends in Sussex because she hadn't heard from you,' my sister explained.

'Guess that serves me right for not keeping her in the picture, but you know I didn't expect to be able to get down anyway,' I replied.

'I just don't think that they really appreciate how difficult it is for you to say when you can come. Anyway, how about a large Scotch and dry followed by a plateful of ham, eggs and chips?' she suggested.

'Sounds like just what the doctor ordered.'

I had only just finished eating and tucked my niece up in bed very belatedly when the telephone rang once again.

'Paul, you aren't going to believe this. It's Christine for you. Looks as if her mother's conscience has troubled her.'

'Hi there my love. Sorry for not getting in touch with you but I didn't think I was going to be able to get down to see you, then the Chief offered to step in at the last minute,' I explained.

'Paul, you are the limit. I would never have come here if I'd known you were travelling down to see me. What am I going to do now? There are no trains tomorrow at all. How long are you down for?' she asked.

'Only Christmas and Boxing Days, I'm afraid. I'll have to travel back north to be back on board about noon the following day otherwise I'll be in trouble,' I replied.

'I just don't know what to do. It's just not fair . . .' Her voice trailed away followed by a flood of tears.

'Hey, Christine, hold on. I've got a suggestion. Why don't you stay where you are for Christmas Day. I'll drive over and pick you up Boxing Day morning then we can still be back in time for dinner,' I suggested.

Her sobbing eased then stopped.

'OK, that sounds a lot better. I'll ring you tomorrow with the route directions. Can't wait to see you. Wish you were here right now,' she replied sheepishly.

'Great, my love. At least nobody need feel let down and we'll have some time together,' I concluded.

Christmas Day seemed almost unreal but the joy of seeing my niece unwrap her presents made up for the frustration I was feeling about not seeing my fiancée that day.

Once again life was about to speed by at a breathtakingly fast pace. Here, there and everywhere with hardly time to enjoy oneself. It seemed that my destiny was always to be on the move whether waterborne or on four wheels. Thankfully, the traffic on the country roads was relatively light and after one or two minor excursions in the backwoods of deepest Sussex, I eventually arrived at a beautiful country house lying in a picturesque wooded valley with a majestic outcrop of rock surmounting a fairly steep hill in the background. I couldn't help but feel impressed. My fiancée's family certainly seemed to have all the right connections.

I was made to feel very welcome by the gathered throng. They wanted to know where my travels had taken me and any disaster that had befallen me.

'Paul, we really will have to be on our way very soon otherwise we won't be very popular back home, I'm afraid,' Christine warned.

'I know. Just when I could sit, relax and enjoy more of your company,' I replied, for the benefit of her hosts.

'Never mind, Paul. We're pleased to have met you. Take good care of this lovely young lady. We've known her family for many years, more than I care to remember. We shall hope to see you both again in the not too distant future,' one of them said.

It was late afternoon before we arrived back to a most welcome buffet meal at my sister's house. We were joined by several of their friends and it didn't take too long for us all to get into a truly festive mood. I only wished that I didn't have to travel back north the following morning. There was no way that I could partake of the alcohol on offer but that was not an entirely new situation for me to face. After all, nobody in their right minds would go on watch at sea under the influence of alcohol. The consequences of such foolishness, from any point of view, could well prove fatal.

However, I did have that journey to make the following day and time was not on my side.

41

Once again, I promised not to keep Christine in the dark as I prepared to speed off northbound.

'I can't wait for you to start work in a shore job, Paul,' were her parting words.

Good fortune favoured me on the road. My return journey could not have been more different to the previous one and in what seemed next to no time, it was day break, with only a couple of hours' or so driving remaining to be accomplished.

'Well, laddie, first of all I'm glad to see you back on board on time. Next, I wanna know what that wee lassie of yours made of you turning up out of the blue.'

The Chief Engineer was more than a little relieved to see me back. He must have realised at the time what a big gamble he was taking in letting me go off but, bless his tartan socks, that hadn't stopped him making his offer.

'I can say this, Chief. You're rated top of the pops, in her eyes for letting me travel down. Obviously, the time flew by but it was all worthwhile. I'm very grateful,' I added.

I decided not to mention the hiatus at the start of my visit for fear of receiving another of his famous 'with the benefit of hindsight' lectures.

'Right then, Sec, let's now get down to the real business before we forget what we're here to do.'

Once again, we followed his pre-sailing ritual of going through the nitty-gritty aspects of who would be doing what and when in the engine room with regard to the operational side of things. He also needed to be reassured that all necessary precautions would be taken to avoid any disasters occurring down below. I was convinced he probably spent the night before sailing making sure that all his lucky omens were pointing in the same direction, or whatever superstitious folk feel compelled to do. All of this with at least three days to go before departure for Oslo.

It appeared that no passengers had decided to make the trip with it being so close to Christmas but as there was cargo available for us to load, our sailing time would be fixed by the loading schedule.

I couldn't help but feel a trifle envious of our Third Engineer. He was a local lad, married with a young family. He had no aspirations to rise any higher in the ranks, being seemingly well contented with his lot and with a real pride in his own practical capabilites as a seagoing engineer. His wife and family obviously thought the world of him, and his sense of humour and even disposition often counted when things were getting a trifle difficult to tolerate. It was not unusual for the entire family to turn up on the quay just before sailing time to see him off and they would stand on the quayside waving frantically as we manoeuvred towards the lockpit on departure, an event which caused him no embarrassment whatsoever.

Just when it appeared that we had become a permanent fixture in the dock, the sailing board appeared at the top of the gangway in its usual location, announcing that all should be on board no later than 18.00 hours that evening, prior to departure.

The usual mixed feelings that most seafarers experience before sailing made their presence felt yet again, but once under way, the sailing routine takes over in no time and everyone normally settles down quite quickly, especially after 'Full Away' has been rung on the telegraph.

Because of the limited amount of cargo on board, we were scheduled to proceed direct to Oslo with only a brief stop over to bunker fuel on Oslo Fjord prior to arrival.

194

'Sec, would you remind the Fourth Engineer when he comes on watch tonight that I need the fuel tank soundings and contents book filled in and up to date at midnight,' the Chief requested as I went on watch the following afternoon.

'Certainly, Chief. Are we taking maximum bunkers or just topping up for the voyage?' I enquired.

'The office have told me to order maximum because there's no problem with draft. Apparently we shan't be returning to the UK with much cargo,' he replied. 'I'm not sure whether the Fourth Engineer is familiar with maximum bunkering operations, so you had better keep a close eye on him. We don't want anything unfortunate to happen, now do we,' he added.

'Certainly not. I could just imagine the hue and cry if we dumped a load of fuel into Oslo Fjord.'

As it turned out, we berthed at the bunkering station during my afternoon watch and, with the Fourth Engineer in control of operations, I kept a watchful eye on the proceedings, keeping the Chief updated of progress.

'Sec, you are sure the Fourth understands that those tank valves have to be closed fast when the tanks are coming up one hundred per cent full?' he queried in worried tones.

'Yes, Chief, he certainly does. He tells me he's done the necessary operation many times before, so he should be OK,' I replied.

'Och, famous last words when the ruddy black stuff oozes out all over the decks and beyond,' he ventured, with more than a hint of irony in his voice.

'Don't worry, Chief, I'm keeping a close eye on things. I haven't had a spill yet during bunkering and I don't intend starting down that path here tonight,' I tried to reassure him.

We finished the operation around 22.00 hours and I didn't waste any time getting showered and turned in with the Chief offering to stand by for our arrival at Oslo.

I woke up next morning to the noise of hectic sounds of activity. I drew back my porthole curtains and looked out in sheer disbelief at the sight that unfolded before my very eyes. Oslo harbour was covered in a thick layer of what appeared to be heavy fuel oil with numerous harbour vessels spraying detergent, fighting a hopeless battle in trying to stop the spread down the fjord.

I shot out of my bunk, dressed as quickly as possible and went straight out on deck to see if we had somehow been the culprits. There was no logical reason why we should have caused the havoc unless something very unusual had happened. I dashed down below just to check that no unofficial pumping operations had been going on since we arrived and it didn't take more than a minute or so to verify that we had not been responsible. But the worried looks on the faces of the Third and Fourth Engineers when they appeared in the engine room told a different story.

'See, there's more gold braid in the Chief's cabin than is good for his health,' remarked the Third.

'Well, Dave, I'm perfectly sure that we're not responsible so I better go up top sides and see what it's all about.'

I knocked on the Chief's cabin door. There was an immediate deafening response.

'Och, who the hell is it now?' he thundered through the door.

'Only me, Chief,' I replied.

'Then get your body in here pronto,' he demanded.

'Before you go any further, I can tell you that it is definitely not us that's caused the spill.'

'You had better be right, Second. I want you to show these gentlemen over the vessel, including the engine room. Show them our oil record books, bunkering sheets and anything else they might need to see then come back to my cabin and then we'll sort this matter out,' he reasoned in an uncharacteristically calm and controlled manner.

I could only presume that he had deliberately decided to be on his best behaviour and not risk upsetting the Oslo Port Captain and numerous less gold-braided gentlemen who had thronged into his cabin. I certainly didn't like the way things were beginning to shape up. The calm before the storm I felt.

'Follow me please, gentlemen.' I took them on a full conducted tour of the vessel, showing them the positions where fuel could escape from the tanks, then we proceeded down into the engine room. I sounded all of the fuel tanks in their presence and confirmed the quantities they contained. I showed them the log books and explained the entries to them. I felt there was little more that I could do to demonstrate our Not Guilty position.

We trooped back to the Chief's cabin.

'Well,' said the Chief, maintaining his unusually polite demeanour, 'I am sure my Second Engineer has clearly demonstrated to you that this vessel is not responsible, in any way whatsoever, for that lot out there.'

Just as politely, the Port Captain replied, 'I regret to have to tell you that we do not believe what you say is correct. We are almost certain that this vessel has caused the pollution. You will receive a full notification of liability. Steps will then be taken to arrest the vessel and those responsible.'

'Shut that bloody door, Second,' screamed the Chief.

Hells, bells, I thought, here we go. I had heard about his reputation from others who had sailed with him and there was no doubt at all that I was about to find out, first hand, what he was truly made of. Ordering his unwanted guests to be seated, he then towered over them and commenced a tirade which increased in deafening intensity as his complexion changed from pink to the bloodiest red I had ever seen. Expressions of disbelief and shock appeared on the faces of those present. Never in their lives had they been on the receiving end of such a verbal onslaught, punctuated with frequent allegations about their dubious parentage. There was no stopping him.

'Have I made myself perfectly clear,' he bellowed at his cowering audience. 'Now get your backsides over to that sodding Norwegian vessel on the other side of the harbour. Get samples of the fuel from their bunker tanks and then compare them with the samples from the spill. No doubt you'll discover something you don't want to know,' he concluded.

His audience beat a hasty retreat to the shore.

'By hell, Second, you had better be right or we'll all be for the high jump and you'll be first to go,' he threatened. I had no doubt that he truly meant what he had said.

We had been due to sail the following day but the cleaning-up operations meant that no vessel was allowed to proceed.

It was the Captain who brought us the unexpected news. A large white paper envelope addressed to the Captain contained an official apology from the Oslo Port Authority.

'There you are, Second. Now doesn't that just show that if you treat people courteously and politely, you get justly rewarded,' and pigs can fly, Chief, I thought.

The remainder of the voyage was completely overshadowed by the events that had happened at Oslo. I felt as if I was living in another world. After all, if the Chief hadn't made such a fuss over the way we were being wrongly blamed, who knows, we might even have been arrested.

42

An air of disbelief about the recent events in Oslo still hung over us on our arrival back in the UK. The Third Engineer summed up the situation in a nutshell.

'If you are going to spread it around where you shouldn't, then you're better doing it on your own doorstep, so to speak.'

'Yes, Dave, one couldn't argue with that. I certainly would rather be under lock and key in this country than most places,' I replied.

Our discussions were interrupted by the appearance of one of the Assistant Superintendents who had boarded the vessel earlier after we berthed that morning.

'Ah, Sec, just the person I'm looking for. We propose to relieve you just before the vessel sails on the next voyage. You can then take some leave and catch up on your social life, eh,' he added, winking knowingly.

Although I had been sailing on the vessel for about nine months, the time had flown by, therefore I had mixed feelings about leaving at that point in time.

'Oh, righty-ho, thanks,' I replied, trying not to sound ungrateful. 'At least someone I know very well will be over the moon with that.'

She certainly was, as it turned out.

'When can you come back down south, Paul,' Christine asked that evening when I rang her to pass on the good news.

'Well, my love, the vessel will be sailing in about one week after dry-docking for survey and repairs, so I should be able to get away in about ten days' time, all being well,' I replied.

Neither of us had realistically imagined that such a turn of events would happen and, for once, I really felt good about things. Probably this would be a turning point for the better for us. The trouble with ships and shipping in general is the uncertaintity about things over which one has no control. I had frequently been the victim of such circumstances in the past and this time I just hoped, that, for once, everything would go to plan.

I had approximately eight weeks' leave due to me but I didn't want to take the lot as holidays because there was never sufficient leave given for college study. I reckoned I needed a month or two in hand for when I recommenced study for Part B of my First Class Certificate otherwise I would have to take unpaid leave, a prospect that I didn't relish at all.

Fortunately, everything ran to schedule and almost before I realised it, I was speeding on my way back to Kent. Somehow or other, I had to try and persuade both Christine and her mother that I had no intention of continuing with a seagoing career any longer than was necessary and, hopefully, within two years I would be working in a steady, reliable shore job earning enough to keep the wolf from the door.

I had been in Kent only two weeks when I received an urgent call to return to carry out an emergency relieving job round the UK coast because of a bereavement affecting the vessel's Second Engineer.

My memories of that visit to Kent are as mixed as one could possibly imagine. My heart floated on high to start with then almost sunk without trace with the ups and downs of our relationship. Two words, in particular, seemed to bug us: if only. They became repetitive. There was no doubt at all that our good times were truly marvellous and that, I suppose, was the real problem. We loved each other dearly and resented the fact that my way of life intervened in the worst possible way and kept throwing us apart. But when you are absolutely certain that this situation is going to end in the foreseeable future, it is impossible to accept that the love in your life sees things differently.

'Look, Paul, this rotten job of yours is mucking up our love life. Can't you see that? Why not pack it up now, then we can get married and do our own thing,' she pleaded one evening, in a semi-intoxicated state, as we lay on cushions in front of a raging log fire.

'I know how you feel, Christine. I feel the same way but, for heaven's sake, please try to understand things from my point of view. I really do need to complete my seagoing certificates before I pack it in. That's the only way I can be pretty sure of getting a reasonably paid shore job to keep you and our family in the style you are accustomed to,' I replied, in an equally intoxicated state.

It was no good. I was fighting a losing battle but I wasn't going to give up that easily.

Once again, I left it to the last possible moment before leaving to return north. I never seemed to learn my lesson but I hated leaving my fiancée. She finally let me go only after squeezing another reluctant promise out of me before I drove off.

'OK, Christine. I'll give things a lot of thought about us and my job. But it's not easy for me either, you know,' I finally exclaimed.

As I drove north, I tried to think, but no matter how hard I tried, there seemed no way round the problem. Would she truly be prepared to put up with things very much as they were until I left the sea or would she look elsewhere then drop me like a hot cake when it suited her purpose? I decided that there wasn't much choice in the matter. If I didn't manage to get a reasonably paid shore job then shortage of cash could well end our relationship, married or otherwise. That meant carrying on for the time being in the same way and hoping for the best. Far from ideal but that was the only way forward, it seemed.

I must have been driving in autopilot mode because my journey's end arrived almost before I knew it, with a few hours sleep possible before I was due to report into the company's offices.

Next day, before leaving home, my mother enquired how things had gone during my visit to the south.

'Not too bad, Mum. Same old problem, though, with Christine. She wants me to abandon the sea now so we can get married and so she's not left on her own.'

'Well, you can hardly blame her. Not many girls would put up with the way you mess them around. Have you decided what you're going to do or are you leaving it to fate to decide?' she asked.

'Look, I don't want to fall out with you over what is a heartrending matter for me. To be truthful, no matter what I do, I feel I shan't win. Fine, I pack up now, come ashore – but to what. You know I've had a promise from that friend of my brother-in-law who's a surveyor with the ABS. Provided I obtain my full seagoing certification, they'll consider me for interview to join their organisation as an assistant surveyor. I might not want to do that but at least it's an opportunity that I won't get unless I qualify in the way they want,' I replied.

'Paul, all you think about is your own situation. You must consider what Christine wants. After all, you've asked her to marry you and she's agreed. Her feelings count very much indeed, but probably that doesn't concern you too much,' she countered.

My dear mother could be very forthright in her opinions and today was no exception.

'Look, Mum, I can't discuss the situation any longer otherwise I'm going to be late reporting in at the office. I'll let you know how it goes after my visit but I must get away now, otherwise I shall be in trouble.'

And with that, I bid her farewell and departed.

202

43

'Right, Second, we want you to get down to Bristol tomorrow and relieve the Second on the *Libra*. His wife's father has passed away and her mother, apparently, is not coping at all well. Looks as if dad's going to have to act as mum as well for their family once he gets home, while she sorts her own mother out. Anyway, you bring the vessel round the coast. The final port is Middlesbrough, and by then, no doubt, the sailing Second will be pleading to return,' the Superintendent commented.

I hadn't stepped on board the *Libra* again since I left the vessel at the end of June 1960, seven years previously, and it was bound to be a nostalgic experience.

The journey across country by rail was just about as demanding as any I had accomplished previously but on finally arriving, I was greeted on board with sighs of relief.

'My condolences, David,' I offered. 'You needn't hang around now I've arrived. The Chief can acquaint me with the usual info. Just one question, though. Are the engine room ratings up to scratch?' I enquired.

'No problem at all on that score, except for one of the firemen, who has difficulty with timekeeping, the lazy so-and-so. He's been warned that if he doesn't improve, he'll be for the high jump.'

It did strike me that the culprit in question appeared to be in no hurry to mend his ways but I didn't pursue the matter any further in the circumstances.

I couldn't resist a quick look in the Sixth Engineer's cabin, with his approval, of course. It certainly brought back quite a few memories, mostly pleasant, and I wondered whether or not its four walls had seen much further action of the type I had enjoyed so much.

In next to no time, I felt part of the team, not just a temporary stand-in. Even the Chief accepted my enforced presence with good humour. He couldn't wait to complete the voyage and take his leave after a lengthy stint on the vessel.

Our coastal voyage included the ports of Southampton, Dover and London to discharge cargo and whilst I was only an hour and a half distant from my fiancée, there was no way I could get away from the vessel to see her. She appeared to accept this situation with an air of fatalism.

'Never mind, Paul. One day, hopefully before very long, I will have you to myself,' she exclaimed when I next rang her.

'That sounds more like my Christine,' I responded, feeling as miserable as hell as I knew from the tone of her voice that she was simply putting on a brave face for my benefit.

I felt as if I was beginning to lose my sense of direction and resolved there and then to keep my mind firmly fixed on continuing my seagoing career only for as long as it took me to complete my certificates.

But first things first. I was determined to take a bit of relaxation ashore, if only to maintain a sense of proportion. I decided on a brief shopping expedition in Southampton as our berth was not very far distant from the city centre. The problem was what to buy a girl who didn't seem to be short of the usual acquisitions of the opposite sex. Although I had a pretty good idea of her vital statistics, thoughts about purchasing items of clothing didn't arouse my enthusiasm one little bit. That was until I walked past a lady's lingerie shop. I stopped in my tracks. The window display left little to one's imagination. I glanced quickly in both directions, almost simultaneously and seeing no one in the immediate vicinity, stepped inside the shop, feeling extremely conspicuous and hoping they had no other customers.

An extremely attractive sales lady stepped forth and volunteered her services.

'Can I help you, sir?' she enquired, with more than a knowing look on her face.

'Actually, I'm looking for a present for my fiancée. Nothing as brief as the display in the window. Well, not quite,' I bravely suggested.

'I see, sir. And what are your fiancée's measurements, may I ask?'

'Well, I'm not exactly sure, that's the problem,' I replied.

There then followed an extremely demanding questioning session as the determined saleslady extracted enough information to help her come up with the correct size. My embarrassment increased in its intensity as I became acutely aware of customers eavesdropping on our conversation. No doubt they were totally misled about my intentions. I could almost sense their conclusions about transvestite leanings on my part.

'Would you like gift wrappings as well as the presentation box, sir?' she finally asked.

The whole exercise seemed to have lasted for an eternity and any thoughts that I might have had about wandering further afield well and truly disappeared. If I didn't get a move on, there would be no evening meal left for me on board the vessel.

'My, my, who's the lucky female?' enquired the Chief, as he caught me examining my purchase that evening in my cabin.

'Hopefully, my fiancée, provided I'm still in the running,' I replied.

I explained briefly, for his benefit, the somewhat chequered history of my relationship with her.

'Seems as if you're skating on thin ice, Sec. She doesn't sound to me as if patience is her strongest virtue but, of course, I could be completely wrong,' he responded.

I would dearly have loved to deliver my present after we docked in Dover. After all, as the crow flew, I wasn't very far distant from her home but unfortunately the public transport system did not operate in such a direct manner. Maybe the opportunity would arise when we reached London.

One disadvantage of coastal voyages was the need to remain on constant standby in case of engine movements cropping up. This meant not venturing very far from the manoeuvring station and telegraph, somewhat restricting one's chances of achieving much else during the watch. Even taking the log required judicial planning so as not to be caught out by unexpected events. Generally speaking, though, the length of time actually spent on watchkeeping was relatively brief during these voyages compared with translantic voyages. By the same token, one could always be caught out by unexpected suggestions.

'Provided you promise me you'll be back on board tomorrow morning, you can deliver your present this afternoon, Sec,' the Chief surprisingly advised me as we docked in London two mornings later.

I grabbed the opportunity with both hands but in my haste to catch the train, I completely overlooked making any contact with my fiancée or my sister. As the train sped eastwards, I wondered if my journey would prove to be in vain. I sincerely hoped not, otherwise I would have a lot of explaining to do to more than one person.

Not for the first time, my appearance out of the blue was accepted with total equinimity by my relatives.

'Paul, we thought we wouldn't be seeing you again for quite a while and here you are. What a surprise, I must say,' my sister exclaimed. 'Has Christine any idea that you would be turning up unexpectedly?'

'No, I'm afraid I did mean to ring before I caught the train but just simply forgot in the rush to get away. Why, is there something I should know?' I enquired, feeling a little concerned.

'Nothing that I am aware of personally, but her mother does encourage Christine to maintain a wide circle of

206

friends of both sexes – something that you obviously know about.'

'Well, I can hardly expect her to live like a nun, so to speak, in the present circumstances.'

'No, but there is always the chance that she could have second thoughts about you if she meets someone else less prone to keep disappearing like a conjuror's trick,' Jennifer suggested.

'Well, let's hope she's around and my present does the right trick,' I replied, trying to sound a good deal more optimistic than I felt.

I rang her home without success so I decided to take the bull by the horns and walk the mile or so to her house, feeling as if my present was going to be more of a peace offering than a token of my love for her.

Just when I was having second thoughts about what I was doing, having almost reached my destination, an expensive-looking car swept by, driven by a young man with an unmistakable young lady sat alongside him. They stopped opposite Christine's front garden gate. I stopped in my tracks and watched her jump out and wave him goodbye. Then, just as she was about to open the gate, she turned, looked back in my direction. Her hand rose to her mouth and she gasped as the truth dawned. Her reaction was spontaneous; she started to run towards me. Dropping my present like a hot potato, I caught her in my arms and we spun round like a mad top.

'You've done it again, Paul. Taken me completely by surprise. Just in case you're wondering who my taxi driver was, his name is David and he works for one of my boss's contractors. He often has to come this way and offers me a lift home from work. I know he fancies me but that's as far as it goes, you know,' she exclaimed.

'OK, my love, no problem, I can assure you,' I replied. 'Anyway, here's a little token of my love.' I handed her my present.

'My, my, who's a lucky girl then. Am I right in thinking

that you've made your visit just to give me this?' she asked, scratching her blonde locks in puzzlement.

'Yes, absolutely dead right, Christine. I'm on a ship in London and the Chief let me come down especially,' I answered.

She hugged me tight as we walked up her front garden path and unlocked the door. 'Mum and my sister are away until the weekend at friends' so we've got the house to ourselves,' she winked.

She could barely wait to open my present.

'Golly, Paul, I didn't know you could be so imaginitive. You cheeky so-and-so. I bet you just can't wait to see them on. Just stay right where you are and I shall return shortly,' she commanded.

All kinds of wicked thoughts raced through my mind as I waited patiently for the big moment.

'Put your hands over your eyes then turn round, Paul,' her voice again commanded.

I did as bid.

'Well, what do you think?' she asked. This time, it was my turn to be taken by surprise.

'Cor blimey, Christine. I'll get locked up for buying you such provocative gear. Seriously though, I can't believe the way they fit but then, come to think of it, I did have an expert assisting me,' I explained.

I didn't recall all of the details of my visit to the Chief when I returned to the vessel in London the following morning but he obviously gathered that the whole exercise had done my morale, if not my morals, a whole lot of good.

'If I can repay you, Chief, in anyway, please don't hesitate to ask.' I told him.

The remainder of the coasting voyage was, for me, spent recalling my night of blissful contentment with my girlfriend in Kent. Surely, we had a future and a lot to look forward together. I just prayed that she would be patient with me, but there were times when I feared the worst.